ZUNI FETISHES AND CARVINGS

by Kent McManis

photography by Robin Stancliff

D1052658

RIO NUEVO PUBLISHERS
TUCSON, ARIZONA

Rio Nuevo Publishers®
P.O. Box 5250, Tucson, AZ 85703-0250
(520) 623-9558, www.rionuevo.com

Front cover photo: fetish by Stewart Quandelacy, rhyolite bear.
Back cover photo: fetish by Todd Westika, dolomite buffalo.
Title page photo: fetish by Clive Hustito, lepidolite mountain lion.
All fetishes pictured are courtesy of Grey Dog Trading Co. and private collections.

Library of Congress Cataloging-in-Publication Data

McManis, Kent.
  Zuni fetishes and carvings / by Kent McManis ; photography by Robin
Stancliff.— Expanded one-volume ed.
    p. cm.
  Expanded ed. of: A guide to Zuni fetishes and carvings, 1998.
  Includes bibliographical references and index.
  ISBN 1-887896-59-7 (pbk.)
  1. Fetishes (Ceremonial objects)—New Mexico. 2. Zuni sculpture. 3. Zuni
art. 4. Stone carving—New Mexico. I. Stancliff, Robin. II. McManis, Kent.
Guide to Zuni fetishes and carvings. III. Title.
  E99.Z9M25 2004
  730'.89'979940789--dc22

                         2004001589

ISBN 1-887896-59-7; ISBN-13 978-1-887896-59-7

Printed in Korea
10 9 8 7 6 5 4 3

CONTENTS

INTRODUCTION

If you say the word "fetish" to most people, an image of a small carving does not usually come to mind. But "fetish" is the conventional term used to describe one of these delightful Native American carvings, even though charm or talisman may be more appropriate. A fetish is an object believed to have a power greater than the object itself would naturally possess. A fetish that has been ceremonially blessed by a priest or shaman would be considered a "true" fetish by most Native Americans. It could then serve different religious or magical purposes. Most of the fetishes created today might more properly be called "carvings," because they are made as art objects. But they could become true fetishes if properly blessed and used.

While many Native American tribes produce and use fetishes, the most renowned fetish carvers are undoubtedly the Zuni, or A:shiwi (AH-SHE-WEE), as they call themselves. They are one of the largest Pueblo tribes of the Southwest. Like other Pueblo peoples, the Zuni live a farming-oriented lifestyle in relatively permanent villages. While agriculture is not as all-encompassing for contemporary Zuni, it remains an important religious focus. Most Pueblo tribes share a similar cultural heritage, but the Zuni have a unique feature. Their language is not closely related to any other in the region.

The ancestors of the present-day Zuni arrived in the area about A.D. 700–800 and by the sixteenth century occupied about 500 households in several separate villages. A Spanish expedition led by the Franciscan friar Marcos de Niza made the first European contact with the Zuni in 1536 during their search for the Seven Cities of Cíbola. Francisco Vasquez de Coronado and his troops returned in 1540 and fought and defeated the Zuni during their exploration of the greater Southwest. More Spaniards soon followed. The Pueblo Revolt succeeded in driving them out in 1680, but by 1692 the Spanish were back to stay.

Americans pressing west from the eastern part of the continent began to pass through Zuni country in the 1800s. The railroad reached nearby Gallup in 1881, dramatically opening up the area to outside influences. Two years before, the Bureau of American Ethnology had sent the first anthropological expedition to Zuni—a group that included James and Matilda Coxe Stevenson and Frank H. Cushing. Much of our knowledge about Zuni culture and fetishes of the time comes from their research.

Today, one main village remains on the site of the old village of Halona:wa Idiwana'a (HAH-LOW-NAAH-WAH EE-DEE-WAH-NAH-AH), about 35 miles south of Gallup, New Mexico. The Zuni Reservation also includes the housing development of Black Rock and a few small satellite farming communities. The tribe consists of around 10,000 people (large compared to most Pueblo populations) on lands covering about 400,000 acres.

Like many other Native Americans, Zunis have long carried interesting or unusual "charm stones," believing they bring good fortune, power, or protection. Stones that naturally look like animals, or even humans or deities, are often called concretion fetishes. Concretions and stones that require very little carving to bring out an image are considered more powerful than fetishes that require a great deal of carving. The reason lies in Zuni mythology.

The Zuni believe that the world was once covered with floodwaters, which left it swampy. The Sun Father, revered by the Zuni as the giver of life and light, created twin sons. The Twins realized the world was too wet for humankind to survive and needed to be dried. The Sun Father had given his sons a magic shield, a bow (the rainbow), and arrows (lightning). The Twins placed their shield on the earth, crossed the rainbow and lightning arrows on top of it, and shot an arrow into the point where they crossed. Lightning flew out in every direction, creating a tremendous fire. Although this dried the earth, it made it too easy for predators to catch and eat people. So to save humanity, the Twins struck these animals with their lightning, burning and shrivelling

Herbert Him Sr.,
alabaster bear

Leekya Deyuse,
Zuni stone bear

them into stone. But deep within, the animals' hearts were kept alive, with instructions to help humankind with the magic captured in their hearts. When a Zuni finds a stone that naturally resembles an animal, he believes that it is one of these ancient stone beasts.

While most Zuni fetishes made today look considerably different from the simply formed fetishes of the past, the core beliefs surrounding them remain. This book will help answer questions about fetishes and the people who make them. It is designed to provide a concise and easy-to-use guide for people buying either their first Zuni fetish or their five thousandth.

ANIMAL GROUPS OF THE SIX DIRECTIONS

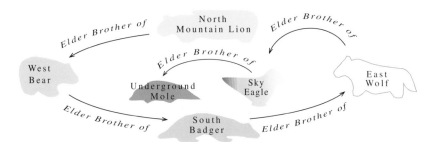

Protective and Healing Animals

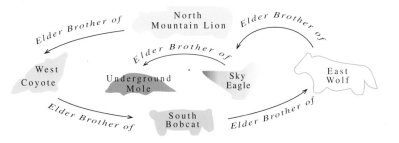

Hunting Animals

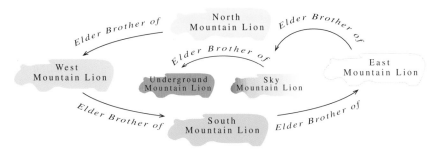

Elder Brother Relationships
(Example: Mountain Lions)

THE POWER OF THE FETISH

The Zuni use fetishes for many purposes. Some enable hunters to catch game. Some make that game more plentiful. Fetishes can also play an integral part in curing ceremonies. They may protect not only an individual but the community as well. Abundance and fertility and, associatively, rain and bountiful crops are blessings a fetish can ensure.

Native American traditions have always recognized a special connection to nature. The belief that all things have a spirit is an integral part of their religions. The Zuni believe that animals are more like the Zuni deities than are humans. They also believe that animals have more power than humans and that these powers, both practical and spiritual, reside in their fetishes.

The protective or healing animals and the hunting or prey animals form two major groupings of fetishes. Protective and healing animals include the mountain lion, the bear, the badger, the wolf, the eagle, and the mole. Each of the four directions, plus the sky and underground, has a protective animal associated with it. The north is protected by the mountain lion, the west by the bear, the south by the badger, the east by the wolf, the sky by the eagle, and the underground by the mole. Each direction also has its own specially related color. The north's color is yellow, the west's is blue, the south's is red, the east's is white, the sky's is all colors, and the underground's is black. When an animal shares the same color as its primarily associated direction, that animal is considered the "elder brother" of all like animals. For example, the Yellow Mountain Lion is the elder brother of the Blue Mountain Lion. This continues counterclockwise around the compass points with the Blue Mountain Lion being the elder brother of the Red Mountain Lion and so on.

The hunting and prey animals include the mountain lion, the coyote, the bobcat, the wolf, the eagle, and the mole. Their hierarchy follows the protective and healing animals' pattern, except that the coyote replaces the bear as the west animal, and the bobcat replaces the badger as the south animal. The diagrams on page 8 help to explain these relationships.

Some fetishes are created with special features. An inlaid, carved, or painted "heartline" represents the breath path leading to the magical power in the fetish's heart. The hearts of hunting animals, for example, are believed to have magical power over the hearts of their prey, the game animals. The hunting animals' breath (emanating from their hearts) is thought to overpower the game. A bundle consisting of various stones, shells, and/or arrowheads is sometimes tied onto a fetish. The bundle serves as an offering that empowers the fetish to better aid the user.

Personal fetishes were often worn or carried in pouches, but now they can also be found on mantels, in curio cabinets, and even in glove compartments. Fetishes usually received ceremonial feedings from the Zuni, the traditional food being blue corn meal and crushed turquoise. Now other foods may also provide nourishment, with feeding time and frequency varying from person to person.

The Zuni also have communal fetishes that are "owned" by different societies and clans. They are generally kept in "fetish pots" of a variety of shapes, including water storage jars (*ollas*, pronounced OY-YAHS) or open bowl-shaped pieces. A hole cut into the side of the olla allows the fetishes inside to eat when food is presented to them outside of the jar.

I have heard countless stories regarding the powers of fetishes, but some especially stand out in my mind. The mountain lion is believed to be the most powerful fetish a hunter can possess when stalking large game. I once met an Anglo man who related an interesting story about the first time he went hunting. Being inexperienced, he went to his Zuni friends for help. They gave him a mountain lion fetish and explained the rituals he must perform for it to work. The man followed their instructions for the preparatory ceremony before the hunt. He then drove to an open area and got out of his truck, gun in hand. At that moment, an antelope ran up, not ten feet away. Taking this as a sign, he shot and killed the animal and completed the rest of the ceremony. As soon as he had finished, two hunters ran up and exclaimed that they had been trailing that antelope for a long time. They wondered how he had been so lucky!

Bear fetishes perform some of the most important healing roles at Zuni. One woman I knew was diagnosed with terminal, inoperable cancer. She was told she had only a short time to live. Friends gave her a white bear, which the Zuni consider especially powerful. She kept it with her constantly in the hospital and after she was sent home to die. She lived four more years with that bear fetish at her side. I met another woman also diagnosed with cancer. She immediately purchased a turquoise bear fetish, since blue bears are the elder brother of all bears. She carried it with her to her next doctor's visit, and the cancer had disappeared.

Beliefs concerning owl fetishes differ by tribe, but the Zuni sometimes see them as home protectors. Several people I knew from the Los Angeles area purchased owl fetishes, independently. Shortly after the disastrous earthquake of January 1994 each customer returned and described how their house had remained intact or sustained little harm. They all said their neighbors' homes, however, had been seriously damaged.

While there are many interesting stories about fetishes, over the last few years misinformation has circulated about their functions. This includes non-Zuni concepts attributed to Zuni fetishes. It is inaccurate to attribute powers and psychological properties of Euro-American origin to a Zuni fetish and claim that the Zuni believe the same. Also, interpreting what other tribes believe about an animal and assuming that the Zuni agree would be like assuming that Jews and Christians share the same beliefs about pigs.

A fetish can represent anything you, as the possessor, want it to represent. It can also have whatever "powers" you so desire. Your strength of belief will likely constitute the most important factor in the efficacy of the fetish. But power is only one of the reasons people buy fetishes. They are most commonly purchased as charming works of art.

MOUNTAIN LIONS

(Hokdidasha)

Peter (Sr.) and
Dinah Gasper,
alabaster

Protective and Hunting Animal of the North

Of all the animal fetishes, mountain lion fetishes have the most varying uses. They are essential to hunters in the taking of big game, especially deer, elk, buffalo, and mountain sheep. Zuni warriors carried them, and they are believed to protect travelers on their journeys (sort of the Zuni St. Christopher). The mountain lion is considered the elder brother of all the other protective and hunting animals. Originally mountain lions were carved with their tails forming a central ridge up their backs. Now they are also carved with tails slung over the back and down the side or hanging down from the back. Their tails are narrow, not thick or bushy.

Herbert Halate, jet

Scott Garnaat,
Picasso marble

David Chavez,
dolomite

Dan Poncho,
serpentine

Vernon Lunasee and
Prudencia Quam,
Mexican onyx

MOUNTAIN LION ELDER BROTHER IS YELLOW

BEARS

(Anshe)

Brian Ahiyite,
black marble

PROTECTIVE ANIMAL OF THE WEST

The bear is one of the most important fetish animals throughout the Southwest. It probably comprises the most commonly carved fetish subject because so many Native and non-Native Americans feel an affinity for it. Initiates of the Bear Clan (or Bear Society) in many Pueblo cultures become members of what might be called the equivalent of the American Medical Association. While all bears have great curative abilities, white bears provide especially powerful healing. Generally bear fetishes have little or no tails, but they demonstrate quite a range of body shapes.

BEAR ELDER BROTHER IS BLUE

Randy Lucio,
Picasso marble

Vince Chavez,
alabaster

Alvin Haloo,
Picasso marble

Ernest Peina, Picasso marble

Florentino Martinez
and Harrietta Byers
Martinez, pipestone

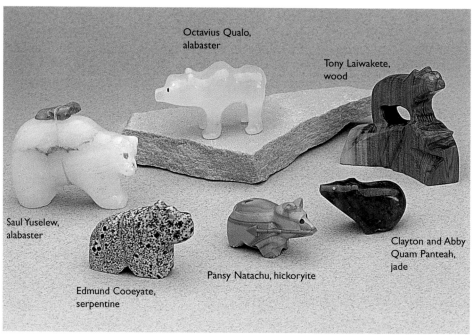

Octavius Qualo,
alabaster

Tony Laiwakete,
wood

Saul Yuselew,
alabaster

Clayton and Abby
Quam Panteah,
jade

Edmund Cooeyate,
serpentine

Pansy Natachu, hickoryite

BEARS

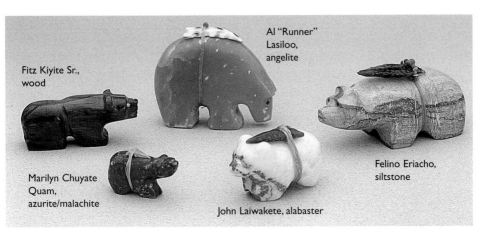

Fitz Kiyite Sr., wood

Al "Runner" Lasiloo, angelite

Felino Eriacho, siltstone

Marilyn Chuyate Quam, azurite/malachite

John Laiwakete, alabaster

Eldred Quam, black marble

Eugene Mahooty, jet

McKenzie Nastacio, black marble

Ephran Chavez, jet

Dion Terrazas, jet

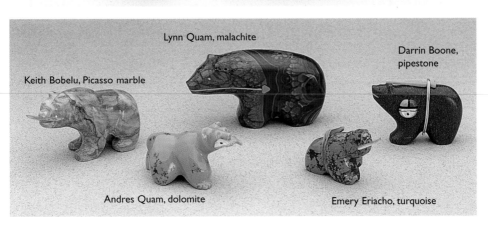

Keith Bobelu, Picasso marble

Lynn Quam, malachite

Darrin Boone, pipestone

Andres Quam, dolomite

Emery Eriacho, turquoise

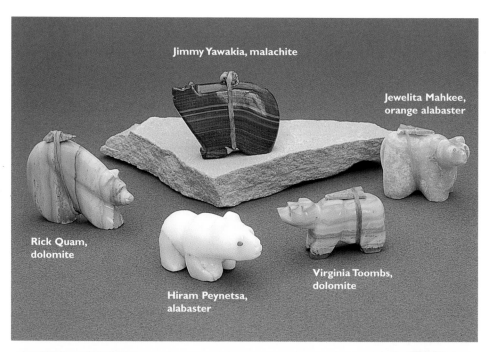

Jimmy Yawakia, malachite

Jewelita Mahkee, orange alabaster

Rick Quam, dolomite

Hiram Peynetsa, alabaster

Virginia Toombs, dolomite

Colvin Peina, Picasso marble

Rickson Kalestewa, alabaster

Leonard Halate, jasper

Melissa Quam, dolomite

Loubert Soseeah and Rosella Lunasee, red "serpentine marble"

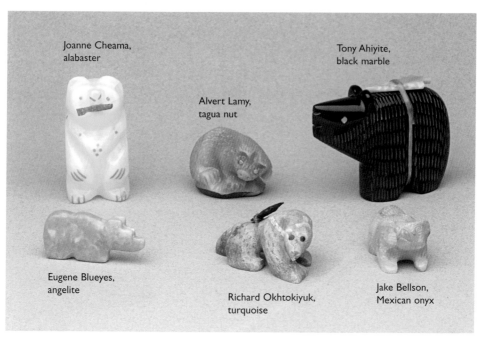

Joanne Cheama,
alabaster

Alvert Lamy,
tagua nut

Tony Ahiyite,
black marble

Eugene Blueyes,
angelite

Richard Okhtokiyuk,
turquoise

Jake Bellson,
Mexican onyx

Orin Eriacho,
tufa stone

Gerald Peina,
black marble

Chris Ghahate,
dolomite

George Lasiloo,
antler

Roger Shebola,
mother-of-pearl

Alfonso Ramirez,
variscite

Burdian Leekity,
pipestone

BADGERS

(Donashi)

PROTECTIVE ANIMAL OF THE SOUTH

Badger fetishes are not as common in Pueblo cultures as those of the mountain lion and bear. It is believed that the badger helps medicine men and shamans dig the roots and herbs needed in healing. Badger fetishes are usually carved in positions fairly low to the ground, with somewhat bushy tails and pointed noses. I have heard the carvings likened to "flat wolves." Badger fetishes at one time were hard to find but now are appearing with greater frequency.

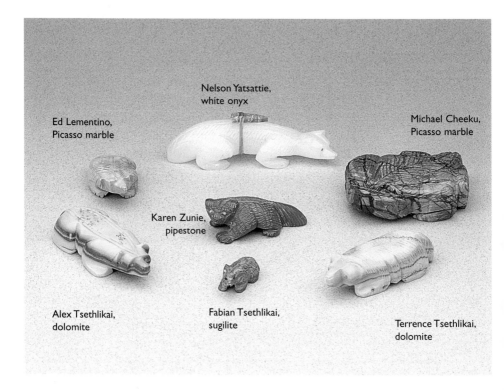

Nelson Yatsattie,
white onyx

Ed Lementino,
Picasso marble

Michael Cheeku,
Picasso marble

Karen Zunie,
pipestone

Alex Tsethlikai,
dolomite

Fabian Tsethlikai,
sugilite

Terrence Tsethlikai,
dolomite

BADGER ELDER BROTHER IS RED

WOLVES

(Yuna:wik'o)

David Tsikewa,
Zuni stone
(travertine)

PROTECTIVE AND HUNTING ANIMAL OF THE EAST

Wolf fetishes are used by many Pueblo tribes. They have very strong hunting powers and may be carried by Zuni hunters when antelope or some larger game are the prey. The carvings generally feature longish, hanging tails which are thick and full, but some carvers give their wolves upturned tails. Older wolf fetishes often had shorter, thinner tails, and a few artists continue to use this style today. In other words, there is a great variety in their appearance, so they are not always easily recognized by collectors.

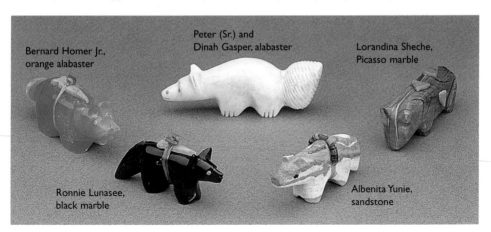

Bernard Homer Jr.,
orange alabaster

Peter (Sr.) and
Dinah Gasper, alabaster

Lorandina Sheche,
Picasso marble

Ronnie Lunasee,
black marble

Albenita Yunie,
sandstone

WOLF ELDER BROTHER IS WHITE

EAGLES

(K'yak'yali)

PROTECTIVE AND HUNTING ANIMAL OF THE SKY

Eagle fetishes exist in a number of Pueblo cultures. Hunters sometimes carry them for success when rabbits or other small game are their prey. An eagle may be called upon to carry a shaman in flight when his spirit leaves his body to search for the cause of a patient's illness. As carving tools have improved over the years, eagle fetishes have also changed in form. They were originally carved very simply and compactly, often with an "x" on the back to symbolize their crossed wings. Now artists can create realistic eagles with upturned, outstretched, or lowered wings reaching away from the body and with great detailing in the feathers.

Elfina Lowsayatee, Picasso marble

Lena Boone, fluorite

Stewart Quandelacy, dolomite

Aaron and Thelma Sheche, dolomite

Vernon Lunasee and Prudencia Quam, serpentine

EAGLE ELDER BROTHER IS ALL COLORS TOGETHER

MOLES

(K'yaluts'i)

PROTECTIVE AND HUNTING ANIMAL
OF THE UNDERGROUND

Mole fetishes seem uncommon among the Pueblo tribes. The mole (or the shrew, which is more common in the region) helps protect growing crops by hunting mice, rodents, and other small game that damage those crops. The mole has the least power of all the protective and hunting animals. Moles are generally carved in positions low to the ground, often with pointed noses. They can have fairly thin, pointed, or stubby tails. They can *usually* be differentiated from badgers by their lack of ears. Although mole fetishes were rarely carved in years past, they appear more frequently now due to the increased demand from collectors looking to complete directional sets.

Aaron and Thelma Sheche,
Picasso marble

Fred Weekoty,
Picasso marble

Clayton and Abby
Quam Panteah,
black marble

Arvella Cheama,
Picasso marble

Georgia Quandelacy,
amber

MOLE ELDER BROTHER IS BLACK

COYOTES
(Suski)

HUNTING ANIMAL OF THE WEST

While Coyote is known as a trickster in many Native American cultures, this has little to do with coyote fetishes and how they are used. Coyote fetishes are rarely found at most Pueblos, but at Zuni they may be used when hunting rabbit. One story has it that mountain sheep were Coyote's designated prey. When Coyote failed to catch a mountain sheep set free especially for him, he was forced to relinquish his claim to the mountain lion, who then caught the mountain sheep instead. After that, Coyote was relegated to scavenging. Coyote fetishes originally were formed with longish, straight-back tails but now are usually carved in a howling position.

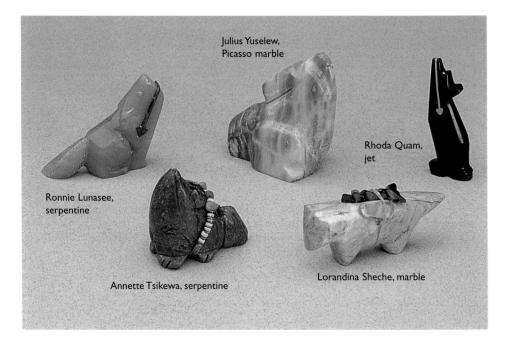

Julius Yuselew, Picasso marble

Rhoda Quam, jet

Ronnie Lunasee, serpentine

Annette Tsikewa, serpentine

Lorandina Sheche, marble

COYOTE ELDER BROTHER IS BLUE

BOBCATS

(Debi)

HUNTING ANIMAL OF THE SOUTH

The bobcat (or wildcat or even lynx, depending on who you talk to) is another uncommon animal fetish among the Pueblo peoples. For some reason the bobcat has been one of the rarest of the fetish figures. However, because of collector demand, that is changing. Among the Zuni, the bobcat may be used when antelope is the prey. Bobcats originally were carved with shortish, straight-back tails and flat faces. Now they are often crafted in great detail, usually with whiskers protruding from either side of the face and having a bobbed tail.

Michael Coble,
Picasso marble

Wilfred Cheama,
serpentine

Dan Quam,
Picasso marble

Lorandina Sheche, Picasso marble   Dan Poncho, serpentine

BOBCAT ELDER BROTHER IS RED

FROGS AND TURTLES

(Dakkya and Edo:wa)

Both frog and turtle carvings appeared in prehistoric times as jewelry. The Hohokam were prolific producers of shell frogs, carving the shell so that the domed half became the body of the frog. Considered a major—if not *the* major—rain-bringing fetish, the frog is also associated with abundance and fertility. While fertility is not its main function, I have heard of women who became pregnant while purposely keeping a frog fetish by their beds. Turtles also have a rain association in addition to serving as links to the Zuni ancestors. Frog and turtle fetishes are some of the most frequently carved at Zuni.

Herbert Halate, jet

Todd Poncho, antler

Fred Weekoty, Picasso marble

Leroy Chavez, fluorite

Clayton and Abby Quam Panteah, black marble

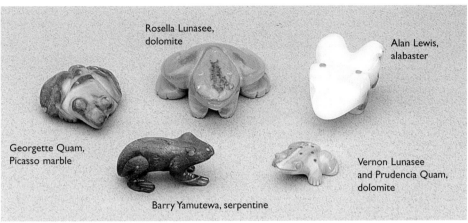

Rosella Lunasee, dolomite

Alan Lewis, alabaster

Georgette Quam, Picasso marble

Vernon Lunasee and Prudencia Quam, dolomite

Barry Yamutewa, serpentine

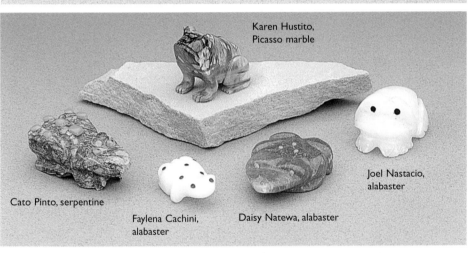

Karen Hustito, Picasso marble

Joel Nastacio, alabaster

Cato Pinto, serpentine

Faylena Cachini, alabaster

Daisy Natewa, alabaster

Max Laate, antler

Russell Shack, pipestone

Marilyn Chuyate Quam, serpentine

Rhoda Quam, turquoise

Christine Banteah, Picasso marble

Loren Burns, mother-of-pearl and turquoise

Darren Shebola, pipestone

Reynold Lunasee, dolomite

Al "Runner" Lasiloo, serpentine

Lebert Kaskalla Sr., Picasso marble

Angel Yatsayte, serpentine

Duane Neha, black marble

Amos Pooacha, jet and shell

Jessica Eriacho, Nutria travertine and azurite/malachite

Dilbert Gasper, black marble

Terrence Martza, jet tadpole

SNAKES

(Chitdola)

Alex Poncho,
black marble

Snake fetishes have widespread usage throughout the Southwestern Pueblo cultures, possessing curative powers for some tribes. At Zuni, snakes are associated with the lightning that usually accompanies our dramatic Southwest thunderstorms. Snake fetishes can be coiled, slightly curving, or slithering. Most are rattlesnakes and are done in great detail now, unlike the simple shapes of old serpent fetishes which were often formed from the curved parts of deer antlers. The old fetishes were more likely the rain-associated Plumed or Water Serpents (*Kolowisi*) rather than the rattlesnakes we usually see carved today.

Steven Natachu,
pipestone

Wilfred Cheama,
serpentine

Terry Banteah,
mother-of-pearl

Kent Banteah,
Picasso marble

OWLS AND OTHER BIRDS

(Muhukwi and Wots'ana:we)

To Native Americans, owls are somewhat like anchovies. You either love them or you hate them. Some Native American groups perceive owls as harbingers of death, while others may see them as guardians of both the home and the village, hooting to warn villagers of approaching enemies. Many different types of bird fetishes appear at Zuni, including birds not intended to be any specific species. Hawks, falcons, and ground owls, while rarely carved, have hunting powers. Many birds are believed to carry prayers to the clouds and sky, asking for rain and blessings.

Bernard Homer Jr., Zuni stone (older style)

Christine Banteah, Picasso marble

Vivella Cheama, Picasso marble

Craig Haloo, antler

Willard Laate, antler

Arvella Cheama, Picasso marble hummingbird

Vivella Cheama, Picasso marble roadrunner

Darrin Boone, cowrie shell duck

Garrick Weeka, antler turkey

Calvert Bowannie and Pedia Nastacio, black marble raven

GAME ANIMALS

Max Laate,
antler antelope

BUFFALO, MOUNTAIN SHEEP, DEER, ANTELOPE, ELK, AND RABBITS
(Si:wolo, Halik'u, Shohhida, Ma'wi, Tsaylusi, and Bok'ya/Okshik'o)

Fetishes of the game species help increase the numbers of each animal so the Zuni will have plenty to eat. The function of the hunting or prey animal fetishes is to help catch these animals. Deer, antelope, and elk were infrequently carved in the past, because the tools in use at the time did not allow sculpting of fragile horns and legs without breakage. Now that carving tools have improved, more of these fetishes can be carefully crafted in great detail. Jackrabbits and cottontails are both carved.

Clive Hustito,
serpentine buffalo

Vernon Lunasee and
Prudencia Quam,
Silverado jet buffalo

Raybert Kanteena,
alabaster buffalo

Rickson Kalestewa,
alabaster ram

Justin Red Elk,
jet ram

Pernell Laate,
antler deer

Loubert Soseeah,
Picasso marble ram

Elton Kaamasee,
antler elk

Ulysses Mahkee,
pipestone ram

Gordon Poncho,
dolomite rabbit

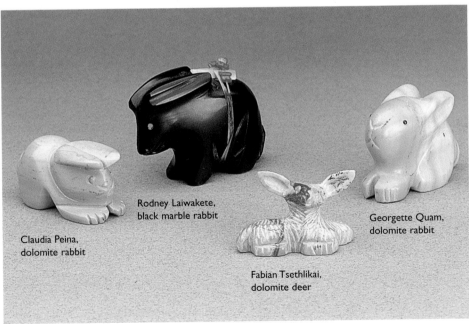

Rodney Laiwakete,
black marble rabbit

Georgette Quam,
dolomite rabbit

Claudia Peina,
dolomite rabbit

Fabian Tsethlikai,
dolomite deer

DOMESTICATED ANIMALS

HORSES, SHEEP, GOATS, AND COWS
(Du:shi, Kyane:lu, Chiwa:du, and Wa:kyashi)

While all of these domesticated animal fetishes are carved at Zuni, their usage is most common among the Navajo (or Diné, pronounced DEH-NEH). Several Zuni carvers over the years specialized in supplying a steady stream of these fetishes to traders who sold them to the Navajo. The Navajo still use them to protect their herds and flocks from disease, injury, and death or to help increase the numbers of their animals. Navajos will sometimes make these fetishes for themselves or even purchase store-bought replicas if necessary.

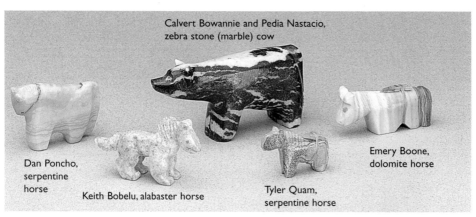

Calvert Bowannie and Pedia Nastacio, zebra stone (marble) cow

Dan Poncho, serpentine horse

Keith Bobelu, alabaster horse

Tyler Quam, serpentine horse

Emery Boone, dolomite horse

Gilbert Lonjose, alabaster goat

Mary Tsikewa, serpentine goat

Mary Tsikewa, serpentine sheep

Ellen Quandelacy, turquoise goat

Chris Yuselew, serpentine goat

Marlo Booqua, alabaster sheep

31

LOCAL ANIMALS

The Zuni create many different animal carvings today. Animals such as beaver, lizards, and horned toads, while often part of Zuni mythology, are not generally "fetish" animals in the same sense that the carvings mentioned earlier are. Their images are not kept by most Zuni to provide a specific benefit or blessing to the owner. Yet Zuni fetish carvers, like most other artists, often desire to try something different and challenging. Some of the finest contemporary carvings in this genre are of reptiles with almost life-like realism.

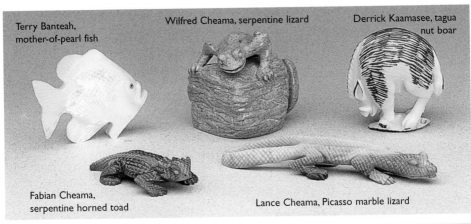

Terry Banteah, mother-of-pearl fish

Wilfred Cheama, serpentine lizard

Derrick Kaamasee, tagua nut boar

Fabian Cheama, serpentine horned toad

Lance Cheama, Picasso marble lizard

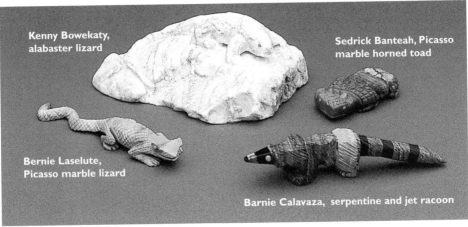

Kenny Bowekaty, alabaster lizard

Sedrick Banteah, Picasso marble horned toad

Bernie Laselute, Picasso marble lizard

Barnie Calavaza, serpentine and jet racoon

NON-LOCAL ANIMALS

This is the area in which Zuni creativity is most rapidly expanding. Photographs and drawings in books have inspired incredibly detailed animal carvings from far outside the area of Zuni contact and even outside the realm of reality. From alligators to whales to jackalopes, innovation and imagination are generating new and different creations almost daily. While these carvings do not play a part in Zuni religious tradition (although non-local animal carvings go back at least as early as the 1930s), they certainly speak well of Zuni ingenuity, skill, and adaptability.

Michael Coble,
Picasso marble alligator

Max Laate,
antler jackalope

Derrick Kaamasee,
serpentine whale

Tracey Zunie,
Picasso marble seal

Kenny Chavez,
serpentine manta ray

Derrick Kaamasee,
serpentine sea horse

Peter Natachu Jr.,
serpentine and
pen shell dinosaur

Todd Etsate,
black marble
dolphin

Lorie Yuselew,
Picasso
marble
shark

Eddington Hannaweeke,
turquoise hippopotamus

CORN MAIDENS AND MAIDENS

(Dowa E:washdok'i and E:washdok'i)

The Corn Maidens are said to have secretly emerged with the Zuni from their previous existence in the underworld. After a while, the Corn Maidens and the Zuni became separated, and witches destroyed the Zuni's crops. The twin sons of the Sun Father set out to find the maidens. After a long search they were found, and the Twins asked them to bring corn back to the Zuni people. So the Corn Maidens returned to save the Zuni from starvation. Other maidens carved represent Zuni and Hopi women. Both types of figures have recently gained popularity at Zuni, and some of the best artists produce quite graceful figurines.

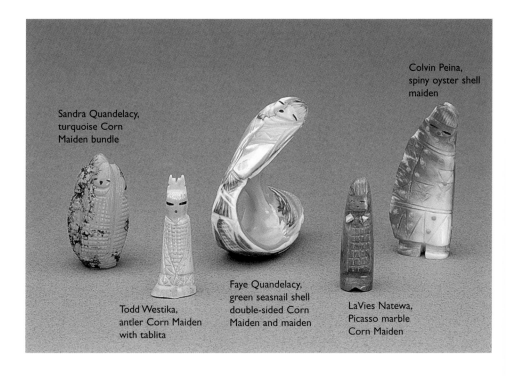

Colvin Peina, spiny oyster shell maiden

Sandra Quandelacy, turquoise Corn Maiden bundle

Todd Westika, antler Corn Maiden with tablita

Faye Quandelacy, green seasnail shell double-sided Corn Maiden and maiden

LaVies Natewa, Picasso marble Corn Maiden

HUMANS AND MISCELLANEOUS FIGURES

Human figures have long been carved for religious purposes at Zuni. The most famous human figurines were carved by Leekya Deyuse, Teddy Weahkee, and Leo Poblano, starting in the 1920s, for traders to resell. Various anatomical parts were also produced in the past as part of religious tradition, and hands and feet were made for sale by Leekya Deyuse and Leo Poblano. Miscellaneous fetishes representing inanimate forms such as houses have appeared quite recently in Zuni and remain fairly uncommon.

Michael Weahkee,
onyx "altar doll"

Freddie Leekya,
Zuni stone Zuni man

Derrick Kaamasee,
wonderstone wizard

Carlton Etsate,
multi-stone
"Rez Ride" car

Rodney Peyketewa,
turquoise pueblo

Orena Leekya,
turquoise and spiny
oyster-shell foot

CARVING MATERIALS

My *favorite Zuni expression* for many stones that carvers cannot easily identify is, "It's a rock." To the carver, the type of rock may not matter unless the fetish is to be a specific directional color (see page 9) or the carver has a special order for a certain stone. Usually the artist carves whatever he or she has on hand or sees in a store and likes. Most carvers have favorites they work regularly. Of course, they try to find materials with eye appeal and interesting patterns that will make their fetishes easier to sell. Collectors and other artists alike especially admire a carver's ability to use natural markings to interesting advantage on a fetish. This is an undeniable part of the aesthetic appeal. A good example would be finding a piece of Picasso marble with a white stripe and carving it into a badger with the stripe running down the middle of its back, just like the real animal's markings. As more Zuni enter the field, competition drives artists to do finer and more unusual work and encourages them to try new mediums in hopes of attracting attention to their fetishes.

The range of materials now worked by Zuni fetish carvers is amazing. I have tried to show as many types as possible, as well as the varieties within certain types. Regarding minerals and rocks (stones made up of multiple minerals), first let me state that I am not a geologist. Hence, I have usually avoided the chemical compositions and the more technical terms for the stones. I think most non-scientific readers prefer "calcite" to "$CaCO_3$" or "calcium carbonate."

ALABASTER

Hubert Pincion,
painted swan

A type of gypsum, alabaster is a very soft material you can scratch with your fingernail. This softness makes it easy to work and, hence, a favorite for beginning fetish carvers. It comes in a variety of colors—white, reddish, brown, grey, orange, and green—all of which sometimes occur together in the same piece. Most types are opaque. Alabaster has been used for carving at Zuni for many years, much of it now coming from Colorado and Nevada. The white type is often used for white healing bears or east directional fetishes.

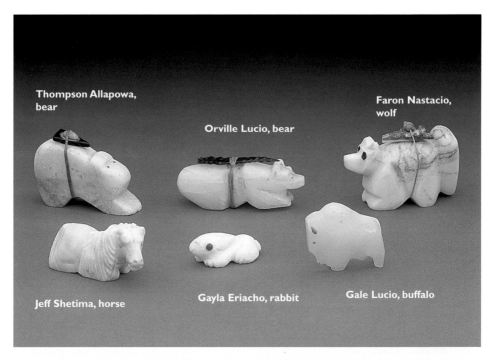

Thompson Allapowa, bear

Orville Lucio, bear

Faron Nastacio, wolf

Jeff Shetima, horse

Gayla Eriacho, rabbit

Gale Lucio, buffalo

Harry Wytsalucy, owl

Fernando Peywa, eagle (circa 1980s)

Jonas Hustito, lizard

Bradley Edaakie, frog

Aldric Nastacio, bear

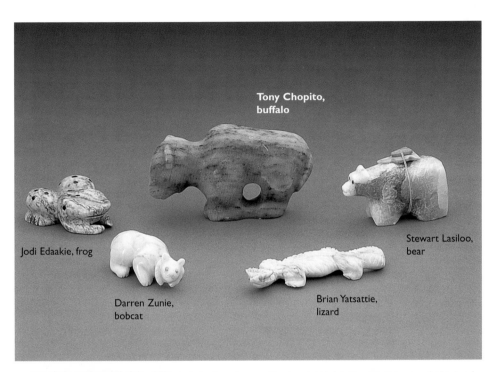

Tony Chopito,
buffalo

Stewart Lasiloo,
bear

Jodi Edaakie, frog

Darren Zunie,
bobcat

Brian Yatsattie,
lizard

Ben Eustace, bear

Stanton Hannaweeke,
pig

Beverly
Etsate,
bear

Chris Hannaweeke, wolf

Lucy Cooeyate,
badger

SERPENTINE

The mineral serpentine was used in the Southwest for carving as early as prehistoric times. It appears in a wide range of colors including green, tan, grey, yellow, brown, pink, red, black, and creamy white, plus combinations of several hues in one stone. Serpentine is popular with beginning carvers because of its ready availability and general ease of carving. New Mexico, Arizona, and Peruvian serpentines are most commonly worked in Zuni, where it is sold under many names, including "fish rock" (a light yellowish green), "frog rock" (a medium-light green with light green splotches and black veining), and ricolite (usually banded grey and green or dark green). Some dark serpentines are incorrectly sold as jade, which is much harder and considerably more expensive. Serpentine that contains other minerals goes by the name serpentine marble. At Zuni, this includes what they call red serpentine and chocolate serpentine. Opalized serpentine is a rare light greenish material from Russia.

Anthony Mecale,
ricolite lizard

Terrance LaRue,
ricolite alligator

Kevin Chapman,
turtle

Yancy Robert Halusewa,
ricolite bear

Vinton Kallestewa,
ricolite bear

SERPENTINE

Lenny Chuyate, snake

Albert Eustace, frog

Jerrold Lahaleon, eagle

Leonard Halate, "frog rock" frog

Tim Lementino, mole

Travis Panteah, bear

Lance Deysee, badger

Franklin Owelicio, "fish rock" bear

Vincent Kiyite, fish

Verla Lasiloo Jim, frog

Tiffany Tsabetsaye, "fish rock" tadpole

Lynn Quam, red serpentine marble bear

Lena Boone, opalized serpentine mountain lion

Benjamin Jamon, bear

Leland Boone, chocolate serpentine marble bear

Frank Eustace, dolphin

Marisa Gia, bear

Wilfred Kylestewa, lizard

Harry Chimoni, bear

Danny Booqua, frog

Jarrold Leekity, turtle

Dereath Vicenti, frog

Garvin Peyketewa, bear

Melvin Eriacho, bear

Chris Waatsa, frogs

Peter Natewa, frog

Andy Amesoli, turtle

Jarvis Bellson, turtle

Enrike Leekya, frog

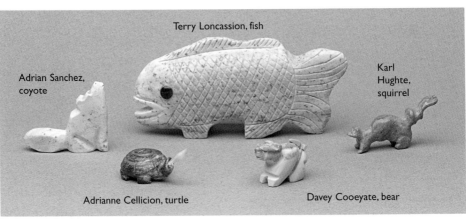

Terry Loncassion, fish

Adrian Sanchez, coyote

Karl Hughte, squirrel

Adrianne Cellicion, turtle

Davey Cooeyate, bear

PICASSO MARBLE

Dana Malani, bobcat

Sebastian Santos,
buffalo

Probably the most popular rock being worked at Zuni today, Picasso marble is a type of limestone from southwestern Utah. Its popularity is due in part to its interesting patterning in tans, browns, greys, white, and black—hues that resemble the natural colors of many animals carved in fetish form. (The name came from the apparent similarity of its markings to the artwork of Pablo Picasso.) This material is relatively new to Zuni and has been used there only since the late 1980s. Carvers can get a fairly realistic-looking result if they choose and work their stone carefully. For directional animals, Picasso marble is sometimes used to represent the multicolored fetishes of the sky.

Donovan Dewa,
bear

Jeff Eriacho,
bear

Harvey Ghahate,
bear

Shannon Garnaat,
bear

Farrell Kallestewa,
bear

Burt Awelagte,
bear

Mike Leekela,
horse

Chris Cellicion,
horse

Drucilla Martinez,
horse

Lenny Lonjose,
seal

Kane Etsate,
coyote

Stephan Lonjose,
snake

Saville Hattie, wolf

Nolan Laate,
bear

Jazz Kiyite, snake

Dana Etsate, lizard

Dean Laselute,
frog

Aaron Chapella, frog

Michael Tucson, bear

Jolene Lamy, beaver

Daryl Shack, bear

Davis Coonsis, frog

Chris Latone, turtle

Gaylen Hughte, wolf

Jon Quam, horse

Michael Garcia, bear

Jay Nastacio, horse

Kelly Lementino, wolf

Tyrone Quetawki, bear

JET

Chico Booqua,
bear (circa 1980s)

Jet (a hard black type of lignite coal) was used for jewelry and carvings in the Southwest in the prehistoric era, especially among the Anasazi people. Jet has been mined for centuries on what is now the Acoma Pueblo reservation near Zuni and is still found there today. The jet now carved in Zuni also comes from Pennsylvania and even Africa. A difficult material to work, jet fractures easily in carving, is very messy, and is somewhat difficult to polish to a high shine. Silverado jet, an unusual variety that produces a "gunmetal" sheen when properly polished, comes from Colorado. Some Southwest tribes consider jet a sacred stone.

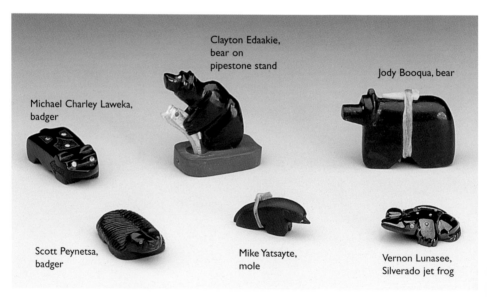

Clayton Edaakie,
bear on
pipestone stand

Jody Booqua, bear

Michael Charley Laweka,
badger

Scott Peynetsa,
badger

Mike Yatsayte,
mole

Vernon Lunasee,
Silverado jet frog

BLACK MARBLE

Another type of limestone, black marble comes primarily from Europe. It seems to have been introduced into Zuni in the 1990s and has mostly replaced the more challenging jet. Black marble accepts a much higher shine and has a glassier look when well polished. It is easy to distinguish from jet by its weight. A black fetish weighing next to nothing is probably jet, whereas a piece with some heft is more likely black marble. While jet may be used, black marble provides a superior surface for sgraffito carving because of its density. The Zuni often call this process "scratching" (see the Roselle Shack, Curtis Garcia, and Emerson Vallo pieces). Accomplished by lightly cutting in lines with an exacto knife or dental tool, sgraffito came to Zuni sometime during the 1980s. One story has it that a trader and part-time biker asked a Zuni to "tattoo" a fetish, and the idea was born. Artisans usually choose either jet or black marble for the directional black fetishes of the underground.

Curtis Garcia, bird

Matthew Kiyite, eagle

Ernie "Woody" Mackel, turtle

Emerson Vallo, snake

Rosella Shack, snake

PIPESTONE

Pipestone (or, as it is known scientifically, catlinite) is basically a hardened clay mixture (also referred to as argillaceous rock) tinted red by iron. It is fairly simple to carve but can fracture easily during the process. The Plains Indians used catlinite to make the bowls of their ceremonial pipes (hence the name pipestone), and most of it came from Minnesota. The prehistoric peoples of the Southwest, however, used catlinite from central Arizona for their carving. Today, much of what the Zuni use still comes from Arizona, but some carvers also use Midwestern pipestone from Minnesota and South Dakota. Catlinite was the first material used for the sgraffito process on fetishes (see Black Marble, page 47). Red fetish carvings for the south direction are often made from this.

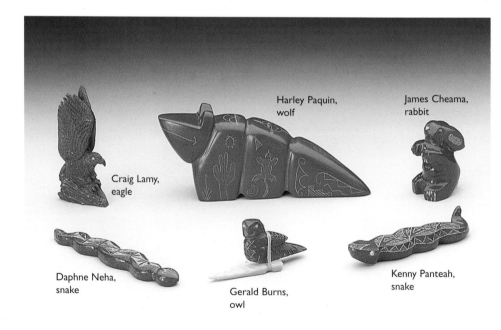

Craig Lamy, eagle

Harley Paquin, wolf

James Cheama, rabbit

Daphne Neha, snake

Gerald Burns, owl

Kenny Panteah, snake

TURQUOISE AND RELATED MINERALS

Sarah Leekya,
turquoise bird

Turquoise is undoubtedly the stone most associated with Native Americans in the Southwest, and its use dates back to prehistoric cultures. While turquoise was worked by the ancient Hohokam peoples of southern Arizona, it found its fullest expression among the Anasazi people of the Colorado Plateau (now the Four Corners area of Arizona, New Mexico, Colorado, and Utah). These ancestors of present-day Pueblo Indians used turquoise in many types of jewelry as well as in fetish carving. It was traded in from mines as far away as the Mojave Desert in California; southern Nevada; the Kingman, Arizona, area; and southwestern New Mexico. The most famous prehistoric mine, however, was in Cerrillos, New Mexico, south of present-day Santa Fe. These ancient mines began as surface finds and later expanded to tunnel and open-pit mines.

Many Native Americans have considered turquoise a sacred stone. The Zuni followed in their Anasazi ancestors' footsteps by carving it and eventually began setting it into silver jewelry as early as the 1890s. They often include turquoise in the bundle offerings attached to their fetishes. Before turquoise became readily available in the twentieth century, this was a rare and expensive "gift." At Zuni, crushed turquoise was served with blue cornmeal as a traditional "food" for fetishes. It also appears in crushed form applied to the outside of communal fetish storage jars. Turquoise is often used to carve the blue fetish animals of the west direction.

Chemically, the mineral turquoise is a copper aluminum phosphate. The bluer the stone, the more copper it contains. The greener the stone, the more trace iron it has. Turquoise can be fairly soft (low grade) to relatively hard (high grade). Almost all of what the Zuni fetish carvers use is "stabilized" or "treated." This means a plastic or resin has been added to the stone to harden it (stabilize) or darken its color (treat). These processes allow carvers to work softer, lower grade, and thus less expensive stones. (In the old days, mutton fat or grease was used to treat stones.) Natural turquoise can fracture easily in carving, but some artists occasionally still carve natural stone as old-timers did. Much of the turquoise used today comes from Arizona, Nevada, Mexico, China, and Tibet. Stones from Colorado, New Mexico, Utah, and Australia appear much less frequently. Persian turquoise was imported for Native American jewelers as early as the 1890s.

Often found with turquoise in copper deposits, azurite (a deep blue mineral), malachite (a deep green mineral), and chrysocolla (a blue or green mineral) are its minerological cousins. These three often appear jumbled together in different combinations in the same rock. All of them were traditionally used for fetish carving at Zuni. Much of the combination material carved there today comes from Arizona, but the deep-green banded malachite worked by Zuni carvers is generally imported from the Congo. Some carvers shy away from it because the dust created during grinding can be harmful without proper ventilation.

Variscite is a greenish aluminum phosphate, primarily from Utah and Nevada, that is much less common in carved form. Additional turquoise-related minerals are also used for fetishes on very rare occasions.

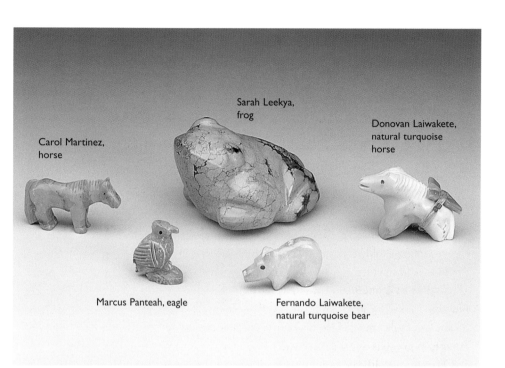

Sarah Leekya,
frog

Carol Martinez,
horse

Donovan Laiwakete,
natural turquoise
horse

Marcus Panteah, eagle

Fernando Laiwakete,
natural turquoise bear

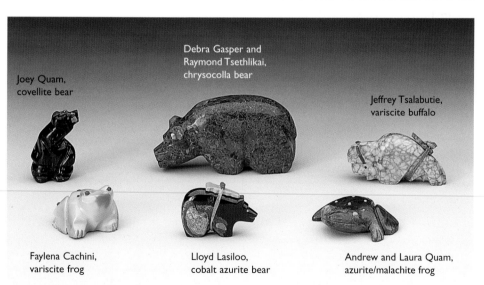

Joey Quam,
covellite bear

Debra Gasper and
Raymond Tsethlikai,
chrysocolla bear

Jeffrey Tsalabutie,
variscite buffalo

Faylena Cachini,
variscite frog

Lloyd Lasiloo,
cobalt azurite bear

Andrew and Laura Quam,
azurite/malachite frog

DOLOMITE

Chris Pooacha,
lizard

Stafford Chimoni,
rabbit

Dolomite rock (another type of limestone, like marble) may appear banded, mottled, or fairly uniform in color. As seen in the examples here, much of it looks something like a thick milkshake with soft hues of yellow, pink, and sometimes reds. Solid brick red (often mistaken for pipestone) is also seen. Dolomite can also form as a mineral with white, red, pink, grey, yellow, or brown coloration. The Zuni carve mineral dolomite less frequently than the dolomitic rock that comes from Mexico and Michigan. Artists often carve the yellowish dolomite for north directional fetishes and the multi-colored banded dolomite for directional fetishes of the sky.

Corey Pinto,
bird

Terrence Tsethlikai,
mountain lion

Ed Lementino,
mineral dolomite
bear

Tony Mackel,
rabbit

Robert Lewis Jr.,
frog

Todd Etsate,
buffalo

FLUORITE

Although fluorite is most prevalent as a crystalline mineral, much of the fluorite used for fetish carving at Zuni is a massive (non-crystalline) variety called "purple fluorite." In this type, yttrium replaces some of the normal calcium that partly makes up fluorite. Massive purple fluorite is opaque, while regular fluorite is translucent or transparent. The latter comes in many different colors including white, yellow, aqua, blue, and brown, as well as purple. Some multi-hued specimens are nicknamed "rainbow fluorite." The fluorite worked at Zuni usually comes from Mexico, but other sources have emerged as well.

Terry Dishta, purple fluorite buffalo

Cellester Laate, purple fluorite Corn Maiden

Richard Epaloose, purple fluorite bear

Donovan Chattin, purple fluorite Corn Maiden

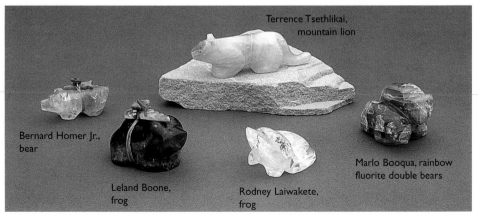

Terrence Tsethlikai, mountain lion

Bernard Homer Jr., bear

Leland Boone, frog

Rodney Laiwakete, frog

Marlo Booqua, rainbow fluorite double bears

MISCELLANEOUS STONES

New stones for fetish carving are constantly being introduced into the Zuni community. Some, because of ready availability, ease of carving, or attractive coloring, become favored materials for carvers. Others may be too expensive, too hard, or too scarce to be generally accepted. Many artists purchase carving materials from traders in Zuni or nearby cities. Stone merchants also bring stones directly to Zuni. Searching the surrounding area for interesting rocks to carve has become an infrequent pastime. This is due in part to the effort it takes to find such stones, which takes away time from carving. Also, the non-Native American purchasers of fetishes generally prefer more exotic and colorful stones. Also, some carvers simply enjoy the challenge of working with new and different mediums. A few carvers, however, are bucking this trend, going back to scouring the Zuni countryside for interesting local stones as the noted carvers of the past once did. While I have tried to be as comprehensive as possible, new stones are undoubtedly being introduced as you read this text. I have listed the areas of origin for stones in common use at Zuni, although the stones may also be found in other parts of the world.

Blue and purple stones are fairly scarce but quite popular with fetish buyers. Sugilite (a manganese mineral introduced from South Africa around 1979), charoite

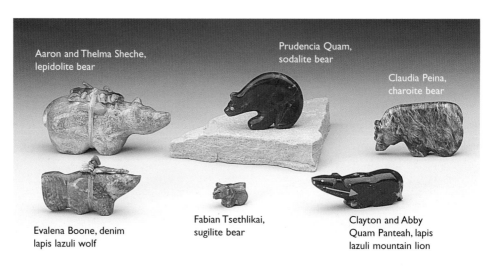

Aaron and Thelma Sheche, lepidolite bear

Prudencia Quam, sodalite bear

Claudia Peina, charoite bear

Evalena Boone, denim lapis lazuli wolf

Fabian Tsethlikai, sugilite bear

Clayton and Abby Quam Panteah, lapis lazuli mountain lion

(introduced from Russia in the 1970s), and lepidolite (traditionally worked by some Pueblo fetish carvers and found in New Mexico, California, and Zimbabwe) are three purple minerals in use today. Lapis lazuli (from Afghanistan and Chile) and sodalite (a Bolivian mineral that is part of the composition of lapis lazuli) are two of the most popular blue stones. Sodalite differs from lapis in that it never has golden pyrite flecks. A lighter blue lapis lazuli called "denim lapis" is also catching on for fetishes. Bluish-grey materials in rare-to-occasional use include angelite (an anhydrite from Peru), labradorite (a feldspar from the United States and Madagascar), Montana soapstone (a type of talc), dumortierite (a silicate very similar in appearance to lapis lazuli and sodalite, from the United States and other locales), and pietersite (a bluish stone with reddish inclusions, akin to tiger's eye from Nambia).

Green fetish materials are quite varied as well. Jade, steatite (another form of talc), septarian nodules (an olive-colored clay ironstone with yellow to whitish calcite crystals, from Utah), gaspeite (a recently introduced apple-green nickel mineral associated with magnesite, found in Australia), amazonite (a blue-green feldspar now coming from Russia), aventurine (a muted green quartz from India), verdite (a silicate from southern Africa), unakite (a granitic rock with pink feldspar splotches), and ruby zoisite (a Tanzanian silicate with purplish ruby inclusions) are all worked, but none of them with any great regularity.

Aaron and Thelma Scheche, angelite turtle

Prudencia Quam, labradorite bear

Dan Simplicio, soapstone bird

Lynn Quam, aventurine bear

Lena Boone, amazonite frog

Yellow, brown, and orange stones used by the Zuni include yellow marble (a limestone variety), calcite (a mineral that appears in a myriad of colors, usually imported from Mexico), iron pyrite ("fool's gold"), brownish soapstone (from Colorado), tiger's eye (a yellow-brown quartz from South Africa), brown obsidian (a natural glass used by some Native Americans, past and present, in the manufacture of arrowheads and points), and Petoskey stone (a tan fossilized coral from Michigan). The usage of all of these stones is occasional to rare.

Red and pink materials are also quite popular with fetish buyers, although, again, most are not common. Some of these include rhodochrosite (a bright pink mineral coming mostly from Argentina), rhodonite (a related but more muted pink mineral, with grey and black markings, from Australia and Canada), alunite (a mineral from Colorado and Nevada), "Ojo rock" (an argillaceous rock found on the Zuni Reservation near Ojo Caliente in colors from light pink to off-white), and Mexican lace agate (sometimes called "Rosetta stone," with its delicate white to dark pink shadings).

White, transparent white, milky white, and black and white stones used for fetish carving include selenite (a crystalline gypsum from Utah), prystinite (a very rare mineral from the southwestern U.S.), opal, white and mottled marble, "zebra stone" or "skunk rock" (a black and white marble from Utah), snowflake obsidian (a black and white obsidian, also from Utah), magnesite/hematite (marketed as "Wild Horse," a white stone with rust-red veining), Egyptian marble (an Egyptian black marble with distinctive white and gold areas), and marble with fossils (a black or dark brown Moroccan stone with whitish fossils—either spiral ammonite nautilus ancestors or spear-shaped orthoceras octopus and squid ancestors). Except for zebra stone and magnesite/hematite, most of these are worked only occasionally.

Banded materials are favored by fetish collectors because of their multi-hued colorations. The stone known as hickoryite or hickorite (sometimes called "wonderstone") in the lapidary trade is a fine-grained rhyolite from Mexico. Similar in appearance, banded sandstones from the western United States (also often called "wonderstone") are also carved from time to time. (Plain grey or brown sandstone was a traditional fetish material at Zuni, but only a handful of carvers use it today.) Travertine, also known as "Mexican onyx," often has bands of white, yellow, red, brown, and pink and is a variety of calcite. Much of it is brought to Zuni from Arizona and Mexico.

"Zuni stone" or "Zuni rock" is a massive (or non-crystalline) travertine in yellow, brown, and grey hues found on the Zuni reservation. The late Leekya Deyuse was especially noted for carving this stone; his descendents are virtually alone in continuing to do so today. Leekya and other older carvers also worked a dark brown, sometimes banded stone from the Nutria area of the reservation called "Nutria rock." These stones include travertine, agate, and jasper. One type of Nutria travertine has been nicknamed "sugar daddy," because of its resemblance to caramel candy. The Ojo

Herbert Him Sr., steatite bear

Terry Aisetewa, jade lizard

Sarah Leekya, gaspeite bird

Fernando Laiwakete, brown obsidian bear

Faye Eriacho, septarian bear

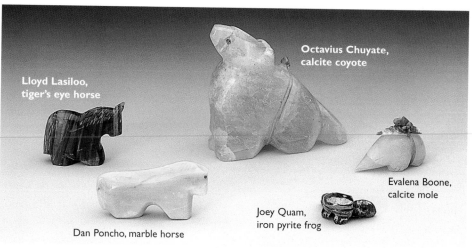

Lloyd Lasiloo, tiger's eye horse

Octavius Chuyate, calcite coyote

Evalena Boone, calcite mole

Dan Poncho, marble horse

Joey Quam, iron pyrite frog

Caliente region of the reservation also has a pinkish-grey travertine with orange and black splotches, called Ojo travertine. It has not been worked much since the 1970s. All of these are now being used by a few Zuni artists.

In a trend divergent from the re-emergence of traditional, local Zuni stones, new manmade materials have also appeared to some extent. While silicon is fairly rarely seen, the so-called "rainbow calsilica," purportedly from Mexico, is used on occasion. It appears to be a stabilized manufactured "stone," according to published reports.

Another rock group used by fetish carvers is jasper (a type of fine-grained quartz), which comes in a variety of colorations. The "leopard stone" variety has brownish spots over a lighter background (from Mexico) or a darker background (from Colorado). "Indian paint stone" comes from Nevada, with tan, black, and brick red markings. (Another stone with the same name and a similar look is actually a clay-stone.) Other jaspers, none of which are worked with great regularity, come from many different locales. Fossilized or elephant jasper from India is rust-colored with elongated golden flecks—or it too may be a claystone. Ocean jasper, from Madagascar, features orbicular (eye-like) markings in many colors. The picture jasper currently in use at Zuni comes from Pakistan and presents golden and brown hues. Dalmation jasper shows blackish spots on a light yellow-grey field and can be found in Mexico.

New materials constantly flow into Zuni. One major new source is Pakistan, which exports large paperweight cubes in a variety of stones, providing a conveniently pre-cut form. These include a red onyx with red and golden banding; grey marlstone (an argillaceous or clay-like material) with fusulinids (tiny marine organism fossils); a banded onyx with brown, white, and a fair amount of green strata; a black and white marble akin to zebra stone but with a predominance of black; vermillion marble (which is akin to red serpentine marble but showing more burgundy red than white); quartz-veined marble (somewhat like chocolate serpentine, but with elongated white quartz running through it); and a white onyx with clear to creamy layers. New calcites, such as calcite with silver (off-white with silver strata) from Nevada and honeycomb calcite (golden with large white veining) from Utah, have also surfaced. New Mexico white soapstone, Texas pink soapstone, and root beer stone (a dark, caramel-colored brown travertine from Arizona) sometimes appear in carvings. A mottled golden and reddish Baja marble marketed as "Yaqui Fire Marble" and a crinoid limestone/marble (with tubular marine fossils on a pinkish background) from China are also occasionally worked.

Lena Boone, alunite badger

Todd Westika, rhodonite bear

Leroy Chavez, painted Ojo rock (argillaceous rock) horned toad

Elroy Pablito, rhodochrosite bear

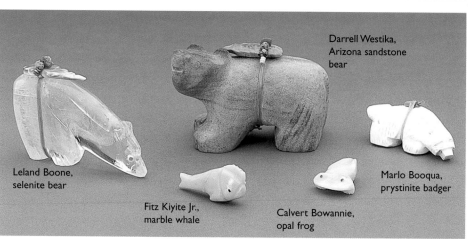

Darrell Westika, Arizona sandstone bear

Leland Boone, selenite bear

Fitz Kiyite Jr., marble whale

Calvert Bowannie, opal frog

Marlo Booqua, prystinite badger

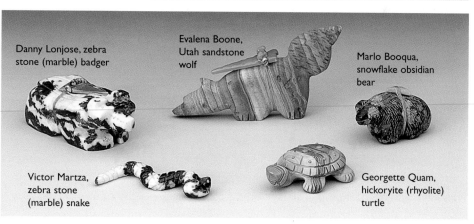

Danny Lonjose, zebra stone (marble) badger

Evalena Boone, Utah sandstone wolf

Marlo Booqua, snowflake obsidian bear

Victor Martza, zebra stone (marble) snake

Georgette Quam, hickoryite (rhyolite) turtle

Francis Leekya,
Zuni stone (travertine) bear

Hayes Leekya,
Zuni stone
(travertine) frog

Jimmie Etsate,
Mexican onyx bird

Leekya Deyuse,
Nutria rock
(agate) turtle

Terrence Tsethlikai,
Mexican onyx
mountain lion

Chris Yuselew,
onyx turtle

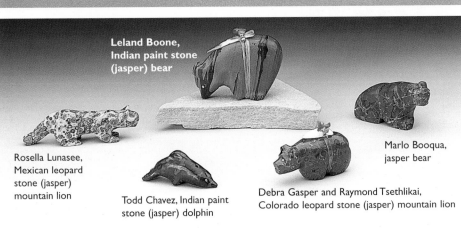

Leland Boone,
Indian paint stone
(jasper) bear

Rosella Lunasee,
Mexican leopard
stone (jasper)
mountain lion

Todd Chavez, Indian paint
stone (jasper) dolphin

Marlo Booqua,
jasper bear

Debra Gasper and Raymond Tsethlikai,
Colorado leopard stone (jasper) mountain lion

Randy Lucio,
ammonite fossilized
marble buffalo

Daniel Chattin, ammonite
fossilized marble Corn Maiden

Brion Hattie,
verdite ram

Rosella Lunasee
and Loubert Soseeah,
orthoceras fossilized
marble mole

Ron Laahty,
Egyptian marble rabbits

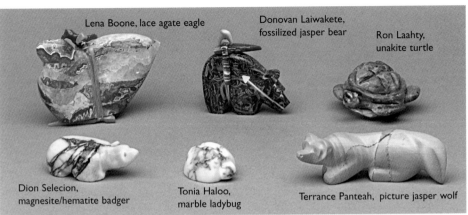

Lena Boone, lace agate eagle

Donovan Laiwakete, fossilized jasper bear

Ron Laahty, unakite turtle

Dion Selecion, magnesite/hematite badger

Tonia Haloo, marble ladybug

Terrance Panteah, picture jasper wolf

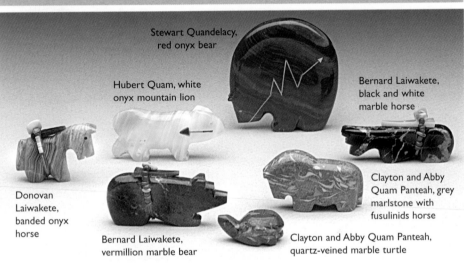

Stewart Quandelacy, red onyx bear

Hubert Quam, white onyx mountain lion

Bernard Laiwakete, black and white marble horse

Donovan Laiwakete, banded onyx horse

Clayton and Abby Quam Panteah, grey marlstone with fusulinids horse

Bernard Laiwakete, vermillion marble bear

Clayton and Abby Quam Panteah, quartz-veined marble turtle

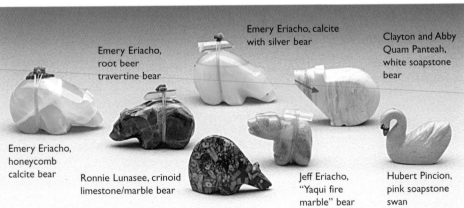

Emery Eriacho, root beer travertine bear

Emery Eriacho, calcite with silver bear

Clayton and Abby Quam Panteah, white soapstone bear

Emery Eriacho, honeycomb calcite bear

Ronnie Lunasee, crinoid limestone/marble bear

Jeff Eriacho, "Yaqui fire marble" bear

Hubert Pincion, pink soapstone swan

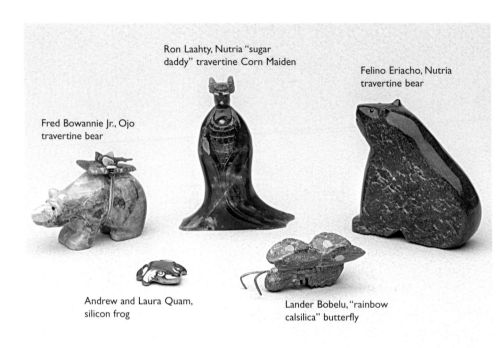

Ron Laahty, Nutria "sugar daddy" travertine Corn Maiden

Felino Eriacho, Nutria travertine bear

Fred Bowannie Jr., Ojo travertine bear

Andrew and Laura Quam, silicon frog

Lander Bobelu, "rainbow calsilica" butterfly

Dylan Poblano, pietersite bird

Ricky Laahty, ruby zoisite frog

Ricky Laahty, ocean jasper frog

Ricky Laahty, dumortierite frog

Ricky Laahty, dalmation jasper frog

Ricky Laahty, Petoskey stone frog

GLASS

Leland Boone,
stained glass bear

Glass is a material quite new to Zuni fetish carvers. Goldstone and bluestone are glass with copper. Gold slag is the glass residue left after gold is chemically removed from the ore. Stained glass has metallic oxides added to give the material its different colors. Among others, cobalt oxide is used to produce blue glass; chromium oxide produces green glass; gold oxide makes red glass; tin oxide creates opaque white glass and makes other colors opaque; and lead mixtures can color yellow glass. Very few carvers use glass to date because of the difficulty working it without special tools.

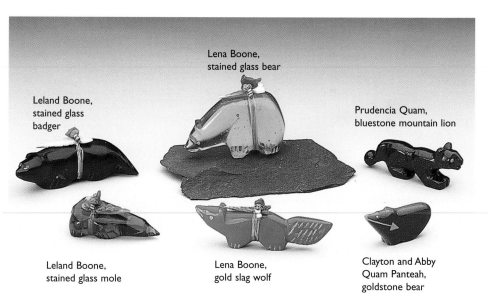

Lena Boone,
stained glass bear

Leland Boone,
stained glass
badger

Prudencia Quam,
bluestone mountain lion

Leland Boone,
stained glass mole

Lena Boone,
gold slag wolf

Clayton and Abby
Quam Panteah,
goldstone bear

SHELL

Shells of different types arrived in the Southwest by way of overland trade routes during the prehistoric period, many from the Gulf of California (also known as the Sea of Cortez). Abalone and olivella (olive) shells were traded in from the coast of southern California. The Hohokam were the greatest users of shell for jewelry and fetish pendants including frogs, birds, and a range of other animals. They also traded their surplus to the Mogollon people, who in turn supplied shells to the Anasazi of the Four Corners region. The Anasazi used shells but produced few fetishes from them. Some Pueblo peoples have often considered uncarved shells to be fetishes, however. The Zuni frequently mixed crushed shell with crushed turquoise and applied them to the outside coating of fetish storage jars.

Fetish bundle offerings have often included drilled shell beads called hishi (HEE-SHE). As with stones, a wide variety of shells from around the world are now available to the Zuni carver. White mother-of-pearl (the iridescent inside of the shell) is undoubtedly the most common. One variety has a band of yellow along the upper edge of the shell and is called "gold lip" mother-of-pearl. Green seasnail shell is another popular material, showing an inner greyish pearlescence and occasional green and

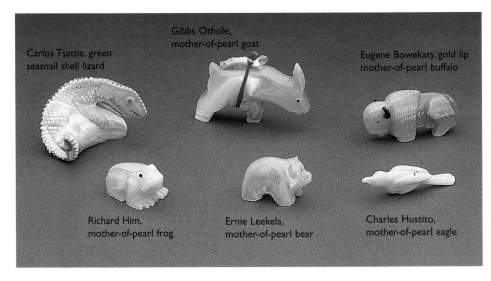

Carlos Tsattie, green
seasnail shell lizard

Gibbs Othole,
mother-of-pearl goat

Eugene Bowekaty, gold lip
mother-of-pearl buffalo

Richard Him,
mother-of-pearl frog

Ernie Leekela,
mother-of-pearl bear

Charles Hustito,
mother-of-pearl eagle

white colorations from the outside of the shell. Spondylus (spiny oyster) generally shows red, orange, or purple on the outside and white on the inside. Artists also experiment with different types of clam and conch shells. The main difficulty in carving shell is from inhaling the grinding dust, so proper ventilation is imperative.

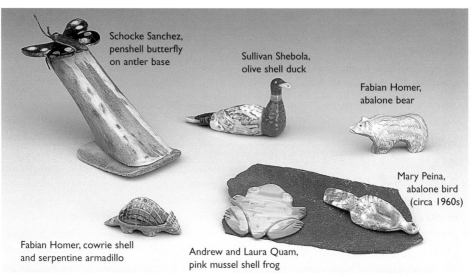

Schocke Sanchez, penshell butterfly on antler base

Sullivan Shebola, olive shell duck

Fabian Homer, abalone bear

Mary Peina, abalone bird (circa 1960s)

Fabian Homer, cowrie shell and serpentine armadillo

Andrew and Laura Quam, pink mussel shell frog

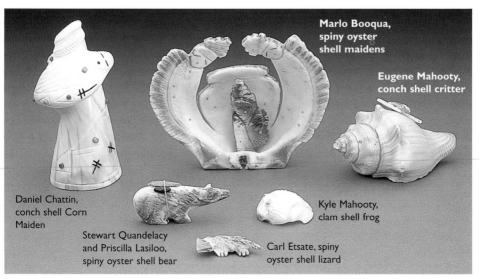

Marlo Booqua, spiny oyster shell maidens

Eugene Mahooty, conch shell critter

Daniel Chattin, conch shell Corn Maiden

Kyle Mahooty, clam shell frog

Stewart Quandelacy and Priscilla Lasiloo, spiny oyster shell bear

Carl Etsate, spiny oyster shell lizard

ANTLER, HORN, FOSSILIZED IVORY, AND BONE

Antler comes primarily from deer and elk, although on rare occasions moose or caribou antler finds its way into Zuni. Some of it is dropped by the animals themselves during their annual molting phase, but a goodly portion of the supply is brought into Zuni by traders. Its use dates to the prehistoric period. Water serpents, animals, and anthropomorphic figures on fetish pots were frequently made of antler. Sometimes these carvings were partly hollowed out to hold offerings and food for the fetishes. Antler is relatively soft but holds together fairly well in carving. It ranges from white to grey to yellowish, often with the grainy marrow revealed on the carving. Several fetish carvers known for detailed animals have made it their material of choice. The greatest drawback to antler is the odor, much like the smell of burning hair, produced when grinding it. Some artists deliberately burn antler to give it distinct brown areas.

Horn of different types—from domestic cows and goats to foreign water buffalo—is carved only rarely. The ivory seen today for fetishes is no longer elephant ivory, but fossilized ivory from Alaska. Bone is carved on occasion but was more frequently used in prehistoric times.

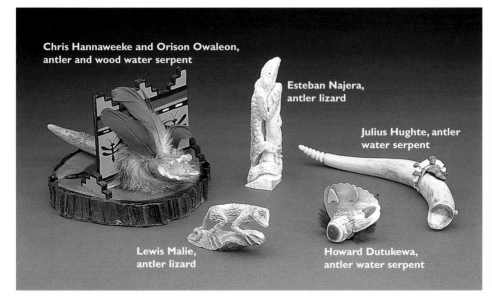

Chris Hannaweeke and Orison Owaleon, antler and wood water serpent

Esteban Najera, antler lizard

Julius Hughte, antler water serpent

Lewis Malie, antler lizard

Howard Dutukewa, antler water serpent

Destry Siutza,
antler eagle

Marlene Waikeniwa,
antler owl

Destry Siutza,
antler ducks

Howard Lesarlley,
antler owl

Elton Nastacio,
antler owl

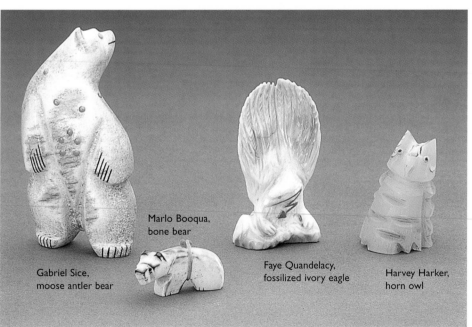

Gabriel Sice,
moose antler bear

Marlo Booqua,
bone bear

Faye Quandelacy,
fossilized ivory eagle

Harvey Harker,
horn owl

OTHER ORGANIC MATERIALS

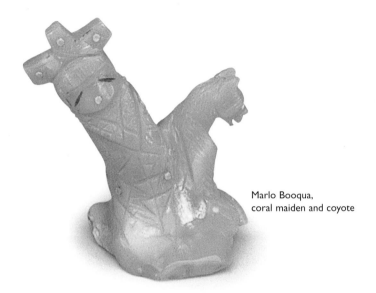

Marlo Booqua,
coral maiden and coyote

A *living undersea organism*, coral was first imported into Zuni in the 1930s to be set into jewelry. Leekya Deyuse used it sparingly in his fetish carvings. Today coral has become very expensive due to over-harvesting in the Mediterranean and is now a rarity. Mediterranean coral ranges from deep red to light pink in color. Apple coral, a resin-stabilized orange-red coral from the South China Sea, currently remains popular among Zuni carvers faced with a lack of quality untreated coral.

Amber is fossilized tree sap imported from both the Baltic region and the Dominican Republic. It is very lightweight; ranges from yellow to mottled brown, reddish, and gold; and may be clear or cloudy. Expensive, top-quality amber often has inclusions. It has become more popular for carving in recent years due to collector demand.

Another material whose use dates back to prehistoric times is wood. Although infrequently used today, sometimes cedar, ironwood, or local soft woods do appear in fetish form. Also uncommon, tagua nut (a palm nut from South America often called "vegetable ivory") was originally supplied to carvers as an alternative to ivory in the 1970s.

Andres Quandelacy,
amber buffalo

Avriel Lamy,
tagua nut
armadillo

Gibbs Othole,
amber bear

Fabian Tsethlikai,
coral bear head

Jones Neha, painted
wood water serpent

Robert Lewis Jr.,
wood mountain lion

Leroy Niiha,
cedar badger

Debra Gasper and
Raymond Tsethlikai,
ironwood bear

Michael Chavez,
painted wood snake

ONE CARVER'S MATERIALS

Carver Ricky Laahty, a member of the Leekya Deyuse family, is known for his whimsical frogs. The examples shown here reveal how one carver can create the same animal repeatedly and yet give each fetish its own personality. Ricky also gives us a good look at a wide range of the materials he selects to create visual interest in his work.

Picasso marble

turquoise

Nutria rock
(agate)

serpentine

natural turquoise

azurite/malachite

serpentine

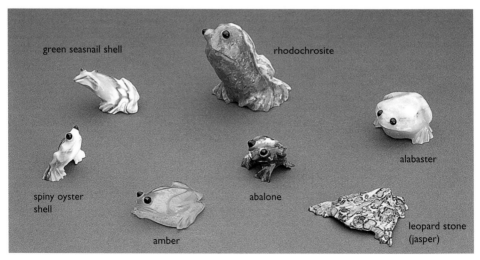

green seasnail shell

rhodochrosite

spiny oyster
shell

alabaster

abalone

amber

leopard stone
(jasper)

THE ART OF CARVING

The Zuni style of fetish carving has changed considerably over the years. Originally fetishes had simple, abstract features. As fetishes were produced less for religious usage and more for sale to non-Native Americans, the public's desire for realism and "perfection" led to a completely new look. In the 1930s, some carvers began to produce increasingly well-crafted pieces, the artist Leekya Deyuse (LEEK-YAH DAY-YOU-SEE) among them. Fifty years later, carvers such as Dan Quam (KWAM) and the Cheama (CHEE-AH-MA) family started creating realistic animals. Other artists let their imaginations expand to make anything from sea creatures to dinosaurs. While some carvers produce more detailed renderings, others have done the opposite, reverting to the older and plainer style of fetishes.

Tools and methods involved in carving have improved greatly, making the carver's task easier. Modern cutting and polishing equipment has replaced the hand tools of the past. Today the stone is first sawed into a slab, if the piece is large. Smaller pieces are also trimmed down by saw. Some carvers draw an outline directly on the slab. Grinding off the stone to a rough-finished stage is next. Most artists now use a rubber-bond polishing wheel to smooth the piece, then polish with a polishing compound on a buffing wheel. Any bundle attached to the fetish goes on last. The photograph on page 73 shows these stages in the creation of a "double coyote" fetish.

Another major evolution in carving has been the growing variety of materials available. In the 1970s, Zuni artists worked in a limited range of serpentine, travertine, alabaster, jet, turquoise, azurite, coral, pipestone, antler, varieties of shell, and a few types of "found" stone. Today artists can choose from many unusual rocks and minerals from around the world. Sugilite, lapis lazuli, amber, angelite, charoite, opal, jade, rhodochrosite, and a wide array of marbles, dolomites, and onyxes have expanded the carving selection. In the past, materials were either found locally or supplied by a few regional traders. Now stone merchants frequently introduce new stones into the community.

Norman Cooeyate and
Jacqueline Ghahate,
antler Corn Maiden

Amory Cellicion,
antler Corn
Maiden

Ferdinand Pablito,
antler Corn
Maiden

Alvino Nastacio,
antler horse

Dilbert Seciwa,
alabaster horse

Taylor Gia,
pipestone horse

The greatest change in Zuni fetish carving today is probably the vast increase in the number of carvers. Back in the 1970s, there may have been about forty. That number is now more than 500 full- and part-time carvers, and it grows every month. With this explosion in the number of artists has come a commensurate increase in the variety of styles. In the past, a trader or experienced collector could usually recognize almost every carver's work. It has become much more difficult to do that today, although many carvers maintain a distinctive style that can be spotted easily. There are several diagnostic traits to look for in determining a fetish's creator. How is the head turned? What kind of expression does the face have? How pointed is the nose? How rounded or flat is the body? Is there a heartline? If a bundle is included, how is it constructed?

The popularity of fetishes has increased dramatically since 1980 because of their spiritual and artistic appeal. A number of dedicated traders and retailers have helped bring about this public awareness. They saw the special quality in fetishes and encouraged their production and sale. This popularity has enabled an ever-increasing number of Zuni to make a living by carving. It has also allowed the collecting of fetishes as an art form to become much more accepted.

These double coyotes carved by Lorandina Sheche from Picasso marble show the typical sequence of steps in the carving process. Many carvers carve without a drawn pattern.

1) Slab sawing for larger pieces or trim sawing for smaller pieces.

2) More trimming.

3) Grinding off the excess to the rough-finished stage.

4) Smoothing with a rubber-bond polishing wheel.

5) Polishing with polishing compound.

6) Final polishing and attachment of offering.

THE CARVING FAMILIES

Certain points should be made about the family trees. It is not uncommon for a child of one family member to be adopted by a relative or another clan member for a variety of reasons. Thus, strict bloodlines are not always represented in these trees. One Zuni may say he or she is not related to another, while the other person may say they are. Whether or not the individual accepts adoption into a family and considers himself or herself "related" determines the point of view. In general I have tried to denote the adoptees' feelings by where they are placed in the tree. As in most contemporary societies, the Zuni sometimes change partners. The past and current relationships portrayed here were what I knew as I compiled the trees. In addition, it is possible that I am unaware of the work of some individuals who may have carved a piece or two at one time or another.

In the trees that follow, the names of carvers are shown in red and the names of non-carvers in black. The (D) symbol means the individual is deceased. (1H) means first husband. (2H) means second husband. (1W) means first wife. (2W) means second wife. An equals (=) symbol means currently—or formerly—married or partners. A triangle (▲) means the carver is shown in more than one family.

I truly enjoyed assembling this family information, as it enabled me to talk to so many wonderful Zuni people. At times it was like putting together a jigsaw puzzle, finding one piece of information here, another piece there. One interesting point is how the definitions of relationships differ from Anglo definitions, the term "aunt" being a good example. You may meet a young woman who is many years the junior of an elderly Zuni man, yet she says she is his "aunt." What she means to the non-Native American is that she is his religious "clan aunt" who helps him with certain observances and tasks. The use of the word "cousin" is also unusual to outsiders, connoting anything from the person's blood cousin to step-brother to any distant relative to a fellow clan member. The interplay of the marked differences between Zuni and Anglo societies and of their many similarities is part of what made this project so fascinating.

I have attempted to show as many fetish-carving families at Zuni as possible, along with their extended families. Due to space limitations, I could not include all of these groups nor the many other talented carvers who are not fairly closely related to these families. All serious admirers of fetishes should be aware that new innovative artists are taking up the craft every year.

Pernell Gasper,
jet and turquoise ram
(circa 1970s)

THE TEDDY WEAHKEE FAMILY

Edna Leki,
septarian wolf

Teddy Weahkee,
Zuni stone eagle

Anderson Weahkee,
Picasso marble mountain lion

The Weahkee (WEE-AH-KEE) *family* of carvers comprises one of the most important at Zuni. Not only does the family contain many talented artists, but marriage has linked it to many of the other early carving families. Teddy Weahkee (circa 1890–1965) was a major carver in the middle decades of the twentieth century. Primarily an independent artisan, he did not work for one specific trader for any length of time. He was known not only for his traditional fetishes, but for his inlaid jewelry, human figurines, carvings set into jewelry, and paintings.

Two of Teddy's daughters also became fetish carvers. One was Edna Leki (LEE-KEE), who died in 2003. Her family is best known for "old-style" carvings. They also do beautiful stringing fetishes for necklaces and some sleek contemporary work as well. The family's fourth generation of carvers has emerged.

Teddy's daughter Mary Tsikewa (SIGH-KEE-WAH), who passed away in 1986, was married to the late David Tsikewa (died 1970). They both produced work for several traders, among them Joe Tanner and the Kirk family. David was especially famous for his fetish necklaces. Members of this branch of the family create stringing fetishes as well as standing fetishes. Their daughter Lavina's husband, Leonard Kaskalla, learned to carve from her family. Leonard's brother Lebert Kaskalla was influenced by his wife's children, Dan Quam, and the Cheama family.

Teddy Weahkee's nephew Leo Poblano (PAH-BLAH-NO), who died in 1959 while fire-fighting, gained fame both as a fetish carver and as a maker of inlaid jewelry. He produced work for numerous traders, including the Wallaces and the Woodards. Some of the finest and most intricate early inlay work done at Zuni was created by this talented artist. He carved in a wide variety of styles, so much so that his fetishes have

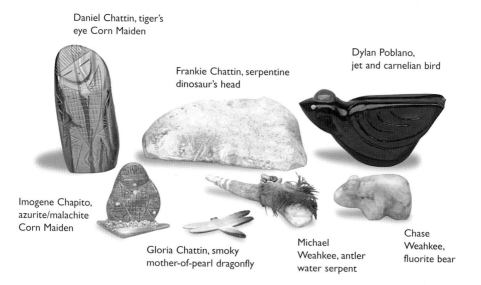

Daniel Chattin, tiger's eye Corn Maiden

Frankie Chattin, serpentine dinosaur's head

Dylan Poblano, jet and carnelian bird

Imogene Chapito, azurite/malachite Corn Maiden

Gloria Chattin, smoky mother-of-pearl dragonfly

Michael Weahkee, antler water serpent

Chase Weahkee, fluorite bear

become confused with and sold as those of other carvers of the time, such as his uncle Teddy Weahkee or Leekya Deyuse. Leo Poblano was married for a while to the late Daisy Hooee Nampeyo, a well-known Hopi potter. His last wife, Ida, worked on many of his later pieces with him. Ida passed away in 1987. Their daughter, Veronica, is a noted jeweler who occasionally carves as well. Her family, including son-in-law Daniel Chattin, also produces beautiful sculptural fetishes.

Old Man Acque (AY-KWAY), another early fetish carver, was also related by marriage to the Weahkee family. He lived from 1888 to 1981. While perhaps not as well known as some of his contemporaries, he produced a unique traditional style. Unfortunately, some dealers have imitated his style and sell these copies as old fetishes. Members of the Acque family continue carving today, as do some of his wife's descendents by a later marriage.

The Boone branch of the family consists of several generations of carvers. Most of the Boones work in a traditional style with simple lines. Rignie Boone was also related to the famous carver Leekya Deyuse (see page 83). In-law Harvey Harker is a long-time fetish maker especially noted for his owls.

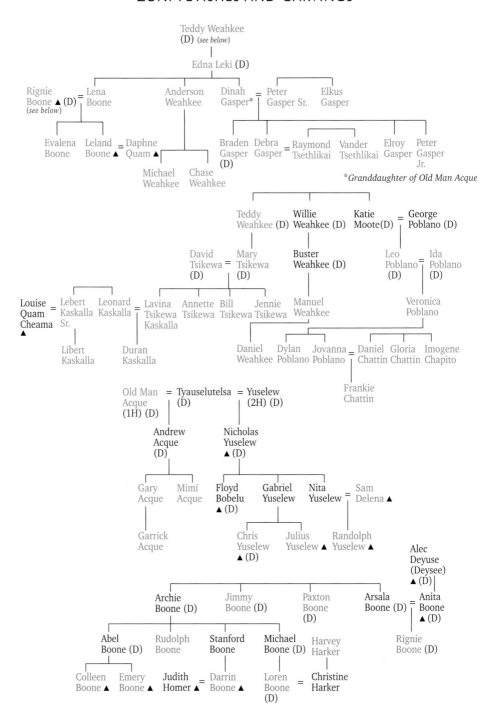

*Granddaughter of Old Man Acque

Jimmy Boone,
antler roadrunner

Rignie Boone,
jet wolf

Lena Boone,
lepidolite wolf

Evalena Boone,
selenite badger

Leland Boone,
jet frog

Peter (Sr.) and Dinah Gasper,
onyx bear

Elroy Gasper,
lapis lazuli bear

Braden Gasper,
jet coyote

Debra Gasper,
turquoise bear

Peter Gasper Jr.,
serpentine bear

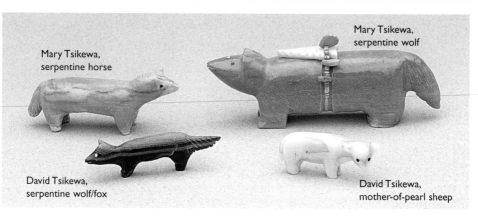

Mary Tsikewa,
serpentine wolf

Mary Tsikewa,
serpentine horse

David Tsikewa,
serpentine wolf/fox

David Tsikewa,
mother-of-pearl sheep

Bill Tsikewa Sr.,
serpentine bear

David Tsikewa,
abalone wolf/fox

Annette
Tsikewa,
turquoise owl

Lavina Kaskalla, pink coral
wolf (stringing fetish)

Leonard Kaskalla,
serpentine horse

Leo Poblano,
Ojo rock
(argillaceous)
mountain lion

Leo Poblano,
hematite bear

Leo Poblano,
onyx animal

Leo Poblano,
orange alabaster bird

Leo and Ida Poblano,
green seasnail shell wolf

Leo Poblano, travertine
(from Nutria) frog

Garrick Acque,
Picasso marble bear

Gary Acque,
alabaster bear

Old Man Acque, orange alabaster horse

Old Man Acque, travertine bear

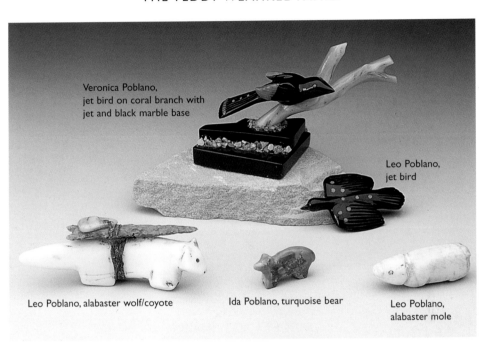

Veronica Poblano,
jet bird on coral branch with
jet and black marble base

Leo Poblano,
jet bird

Leo Poblano, alabaster wolf/coyote

Ida Poblano, turquoise bear

Leo Poblano,
alabaster mole

Harvey Harker,
antler owl (circa 1970s)

Manuel Weahkee,
serpentine bear

Mimi Acque,
pipestone bear

Randolph Yuselew, serpentine lizard

Harvey Harker,
antler fish

Daniel Weahkee,
antler badger

Teddy Weahkee,
Zuni stone (travertine) bear

Jennie Tsikewa,
angelite bear

Elkus Gasper,
serpentine bear
(circa 1980s)

Rignie and Lena Boone,
turquoise wolf
(circa 1970s)

Daphne Quam,
serpentine turtle

Vander Tsethlikai,
pipestone bear

Libert Kaskalla,
serpentine lizard

David Tsikewa,
mother-of-pearl goat (circa 1960s)

David Tsikewa,
turquoise frog
(circa 1960s)

Duran Kaskalla, serpentine bear

Lavina Kaskalla, alabaster bear

Lebert Kaskalla Sr.,
serpentine bear

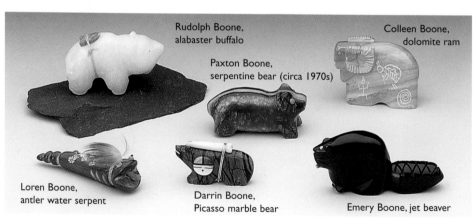

Rudolph Boone,
alabaster buffalo

Colleen Boone,
dolomite ram

Paxton Boone,
serpentine bear (circa 1970s)

Loren Boone,
antler water serpent

Darrin Boone,
Picasso marble bear

Emery Boone, jet beaver

82

THE LEEKYA DEYUSE FAMILY

Leekya Deyuse,
travertine sheep

Leekya Deyuse (LEEK-YAH DAY-YOU-SEE) was probably the most famous fetish carver in the history of Zuni. He was born in 1889 and worked for many years for noted Zuni traders C. G. Wallace, the Kirk family, and others, producing some of the finest carvings in Zuni up to that time. He also created beautiful fetish necklaces, human figurines, and pieces set into jewelry, including leaves, animals, birds, and hands. His carvings became even more refined after he began using better equipment later in life. He died in 1966, but his artistry continues to appear in countless books, magazines, and museums. His is the one name known by people not overly familiar with Zuni fetishes. His work brings some of the highest prices on the "old" fetish market, even though it can be recognized only by style and not by signature. Because of the value and popularity of Leekya's work, fakes are not uncommon. Carvings by members of his family are often sold, intentionally or unintentionally, as his. While certainly influenced by Leekya, their works are different creations and should be appreciated in their own right. Sarah is the last of Leekya's children still making fetishes, but the fourth generation of carvers in this family is now active.

Leekya Deyuse's niece Sadie (died 1990) married Morris Laahty (LAY-AH-TEE), a talented inlay jeweler born in 1924 who on very rare occasions would show off his lapidary prowess by carving fetishes. He passed away in 1987, but his son Ricky carries on the tradition. Leekya's daughter Alice (died 1988) married Bernard Homer Sr. Their children also carve in the traditional rounded family style. In the Homer family, Lambert Sr. and Lambert Jr. were excellent inlay artists but rarely carved fetishes. Several of Lambert Jr.'s children work in a range of styles.

A number of descendents from Francis Leekya (died 2003) carve in the old family style, often in Zuni stone (travertine) from the reservation area.

Deysee is an alternate spelling for some family members.

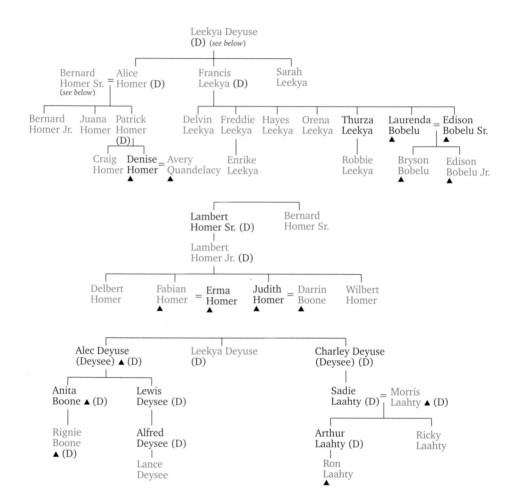

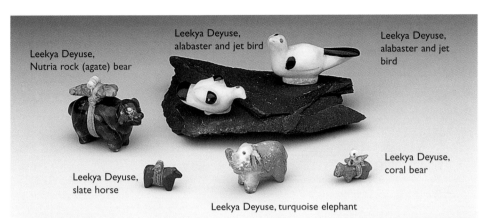

Leekya Deyuse, Nutria rock (agate) bear

Leekya Deyuse, alabaster and jet bird

Leekya Deyuse, alabaster and jet bird

Leekya Deyuse, slate horse

Leekya Deyuse, turquoise elephant

Leekya Deyuse, coral bear

Hayes Leekya, Zuni stone (travertine) "priest figure"

Bryson Bobelu, Picasso marble bear

Freddie Leekya, Zuni stone (travertine) bear

Edison Bobelu Jr., jet bird

Robbie Leekya, Zuni stone (travertine) bear

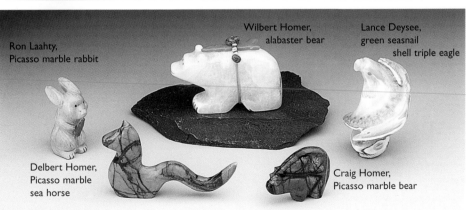

Ron Laahty, Picasso marble rabbit

Wilbert Homer, alabaster bear

Lance Deysee, green seasnail shell triple eagle

Delbert Homer, Picasso marble sea horse

Craig Homer, Picasso marble bear

ZUNI FETISHES AND CARVINGS

Leekya Deyuse,
Zuni stone bear

Leekya Deyuse, coral snake

Morris Laahty,
serpentine frog

Leekya Deyuse,
turquoise frog

Leekya Deyuse,
abalone horse

Ricky Laahty,
serpentine frog

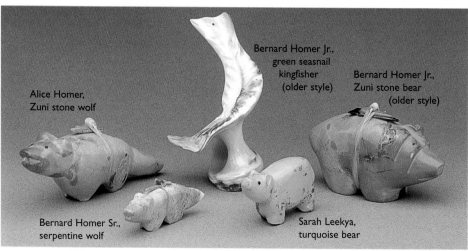

Alice Homer,
Zuni stone wolf

Bernard Homer Jr.,
green seasnail
kingfisher
(older style)

Bernard Homer Jr.,
Zuni stone bear
(older style)

Bernard Homer Sr.,
serpentine wolf

Sarah Leekya,
turquoise bear

Pat Homer,
Zuni stone bear

Francis Leekya,
serpentine bear

Juana Homer,
marble bear

Delvin Leekya,
dolomite bear

Fabian Homer,
serpentine and
shell turtle

THE THEODORE KUCATE FAMILY

Theodore Kucate,
travertine bobcat

Theodore Kucate (COO-KAH-TEE) was a recognized early carver at Zuni but was probably best known for the family's traditional dance troupe. His carvings, while also very traditional, had a charming friendliness to them. Born about 1888, he died in 1980.

Theodore's family continues to be very active in fetish carving, basing most of their work on pieces shown in Cushing's *Zuni Fetiches*. Both Theodore's and son-in-law Aaron Sheche's (SHEE-SHEE, died 2002) older-style carvings are often copied by unscrupulous dealers and sold as old fetishes. These fakes are rarely attributed to any specific carver. Today the family's style is very homogeneous. It seems difficult to tell one family member's carving from another's unless initials are on the bottom of the piece. All of their work is pleasing.

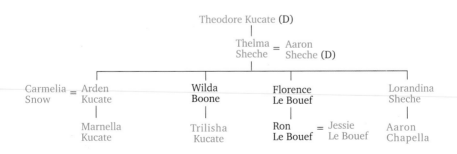

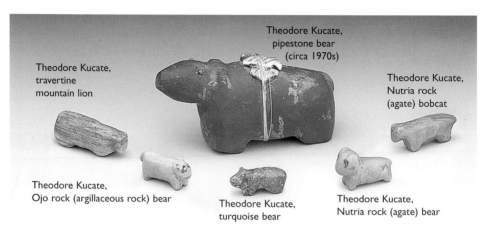

Theodore Kucate,
pipestone bear
(circa 1970s)

Theodore Kucate,
travertine
mountain lion

Theodore Kucate,
Nutria rock
(agate) bobcat

Theodore Kucate,
Ojo rock (argillaceous rock) bear

Theodore Kucate,
turquoise bear

Theodore Kucate,
Nutria rock (agate) bear

Theodore Kucate,
sandstone mountain lion

Theodore Kucate,
Ojo rock horse

Aaron Sheche,
travertine bear
(older style)

Theodore Kucate,
alabaster bear

Aaron and Thelma Sheche,
serpentine double coyotes

Carmelia Snow,
black marble wolf

Lorandina Sheche,
septarian double
mountain lions

Jessie LeBouef,
Picasso
marble eagle

Marnella Kucate,
angelite double eagles

Trilisha Kucate, serpentine double coyotes

THE QUANDELACY FAMILY

Andres Quandelacy,
amber wolf

The Quandelacy (KWAN-DEH-LAY-SEE) *family* creates some of the most elegant fetishes in Zuni. The late Ellen Quandelacy (died 2002) learned the art of carving from her father, Johnny Quam. Her children took up fetish carving with a passion and produce a wide range of work from traditional to modern stylings.

Stewart Quandelacy's bears have almost become the quintessential Zuni fetish. This family's artistry has helped set the standard for much of contemporary fetish carving with their clean lines and excellent finishing. Cousin Faye Quam studied carving with Mary Tsikewa (see page 76).

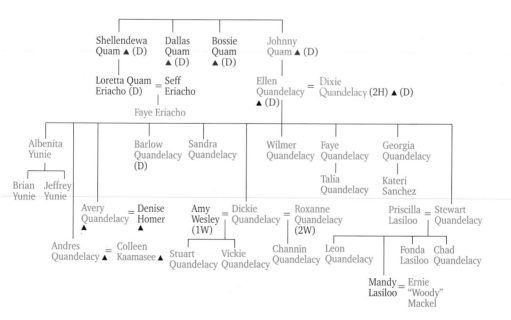

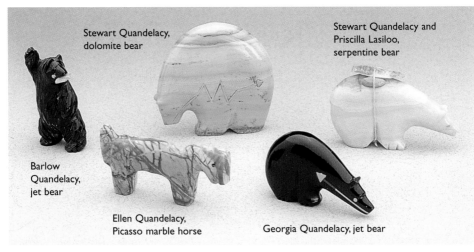

Stewart Quandelacy, dolomite bear

Stewart Quandelacy and Priscilla Lasiloo, serpentine bear

Barlow Quandelacy, jet bear

Ellen Quandelacy, Picasso marble horse

Georgia Quandelacy, jet bear

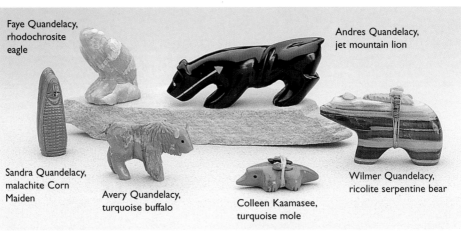

Faye Quandelacy, rhodochrosite eagle

Andres Quandelacy, jet mountain lion

Sandra Quandelacy, malachite Corn Maiden

Avery Quandelacy, turquoise buffalo

Colleen Kaamasee, turquoise mole

Wilmer Quandelacy, ricolite serpentine bear

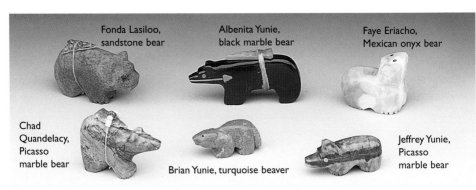

Fonda Lasiloo, sandstone bear

Albenita Yunie, black marble bear

Faye Eriacho, Mexican onyx bear

Chad Quandelacy, Picasso marble bear

Brian Yunie, turquoise beaver

Jeffrey Yunie, Picasso marble bear

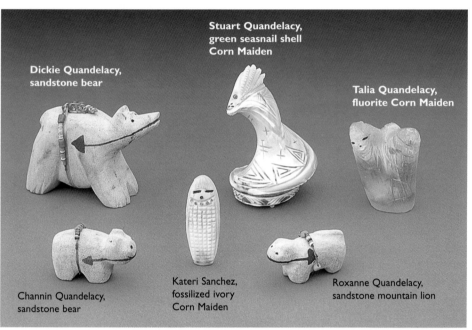

Stuart Quandelacy,
green seasnail shell
Corn Maiden

Dickie Quandelacy,
sandstone bear

Talia Quandelacy,
fluorite Corn Maiden

Channin Quandelacy,
sandstone bear

Kateri Sanchez,
fossilized ivory
Corn Maiden

Roxanne Quandelacy,
sandstone mountain lion

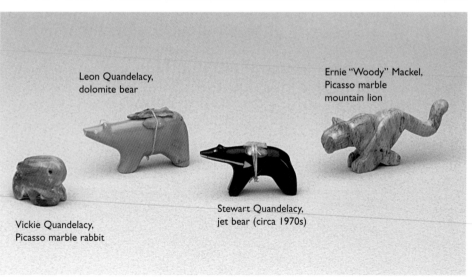

Leon Quandelacy,
dolomite bear

Ernie "Woody" Mackel,
Picasso marble
mountain lion

Vickie Quandelacy,
Picasso marble rabbit

Stewart Quandelacy,
jet bear (circa 1970s)

THE GEORGE HALOO CHEECHEE FAMILY

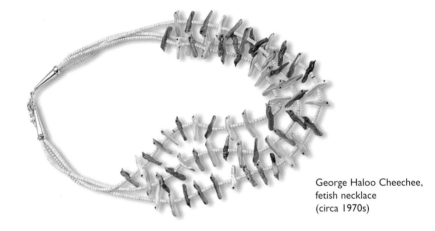

George Haloo Cheechee,
fetish necklace
(circa 1970s)

George Haloo (HAH-LOO) *Cheechee* is one of the most important figures in Zuni fetish carving. He passed on his knowledge to his extended family, who in turn shared it with their families, relatives, and friends. Many other carving families first learned from George or one of his descendents. He started carving in the 1930s and was known for his fetish necklaces, distinguished by the slightly turned heads of his animals. George died in 1983. He taught his daughter Lita Delena (DEH-LEE-NAH), who passed away in 2003. Lita and her husband, Sam, produced their own unique style of fetish necklaces starting in the 1960s. A few carvers on this side of the family create standing fetishes, but most were instructed in the making of stringing fetishes by Sam and Lita. Some, such as Barry Yamutewa (YAH-MOO-TEE-WAH), create both.

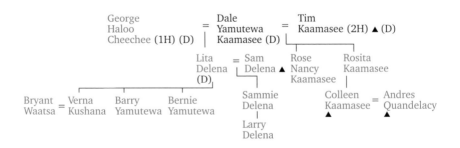

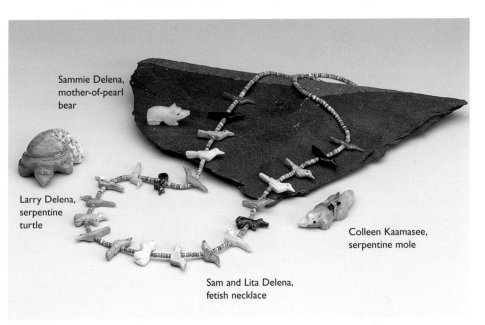

Sammie Delena,
mother-of-pearl
bear

Larry Delena,
serpentine
turtle

Colleen Kaamasee,
serpentine mole

Sam and Lita Delena,
fetish necklace

Rosita Kaamasee,
turquoise duck

Bernie Yamutewa,
malachite turtle

Barry Yamutewa,
Picasso marble
badger

Bryant Waatsa,
turquoise fish

Verna Kushana,
malachite fish

Rose Nancy Kaamasee,
turquoise frog

THE HALOO FAMILY

Raymond "Ramie" Haloo,
antler bear (circa 1980s)

Raymond "Ramie" Haloo,
antler bear

Miguel Haloo,
antler bear (circa 1980s)

This branch of the family is descended from George Haloo Cheechee and his second wife, Naomi Haloo. Their daughter Tina Sice (rhymes with ICE) has recently followed in George's footsteps by producing stringing fetishes. Her late brother Miguel Haloo started carving in the late 1970s and initiated the famous standing-bear style often associated with this family. He passed away in 1990, after teaching many in the later generations to carve. Colvin Peina (PAY-NA) was the first carver of the younger generation who started working in the mid 1980s and has also influenced others. The late Jacob Haloo (George's brother) had several children who are exceptional jewelers, while some descendents are also fetish carvers. In addition to the standing bears, some family members are also known for Corn Maidens.

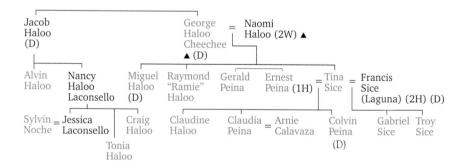

Jacob Haloo (D)

George Haloo Cheechee ▲ (D) = Naomi Haloo (2W) ▲

Alvin Haloo — Nancy Haloo Laconsello

Miguel Haloo (D)

Raymond "Ramie" Haloo

Gerald Peina

Ernest Peina (1H) = Tina Sice = Francis Sice (Laguna) (2H) (D)

Sylvin Noche = Jessica Laconsello

Craig Haloo

Claudine Haloo

Claudia Peina = Arnie Calavaza

Colvin Peina (D)

Gabriel Sice   Troy Sice

Tonia Haloo

THE HALOO FAMILY

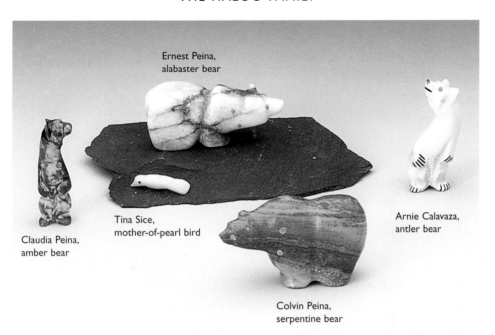

Ernest Peina,
alabaster bear

Arnie Calavaza,
antler bear

Tina Sice,
mother-of-pearl bird

Claudia Peina,
amber bear

Colvin Peina,
serpentine bear

Craig Haloo,
antler owl

Troy Sice,
antler Corn
Maiden

Gabriel Sice,
antler Corn
Maiden

Sylvin Noche,
alabaster owl

Alvin Haloo,
Picasso marble wolf

Claudine Haloo,
Picasso marble bear

THE ANDREW EMERSON QUAM AND BOSSIE QUAM FAMILIES

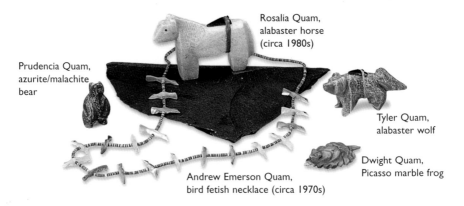

Rosalia Quam, alabaster horse (circa 1980s)

Prudencia Quam, azurite/malachite bear

Tyler Quam, alabaster wolf

Dwight Quam, Picasso marble frog

Andrew Emerson Quam, bird fetish necklace (circa 1970s)

George Haloo Cheechee's stepdaughter, the late Rosalia Quam (KWAM), who died in 1989, was known for stringing bird fetishes and for her fetish horses, inlaid frogs, and owls. Both she and her late husband Andrew Emerson Quam (who died in 1976) taught their children the art, as George Haloo Cheechee had taught her. Andrew Emerson was famous for his bird fetish necklaces. The current Quam generation produces a wide range of styles, from fairly realistic to more abstract. Some members are known for specific animals, as Andres Quam for bears or Andrew and Laura Quam for frogs and turtles. Others, such as Prudencia and Tyler Quam, have produced a multiplicity of creatures. Interestingly, the Mahkee (MAH-KEE) sisters Jewelita and Laura have married two of the Quam brothers—Andres and Andrew. Not surprisingly, the sisters and their brother Ulysses have learned fetish carving from the Quams.

Andrew Emerson Quam's nieces and nephews create some carvings as well. The Burnses primarily practice the art of sgraffito on their pieces. Andrew Emerson first helped Gabriel start in the late 1970s. The Burns family members and cousins Emery and Colleen Boone prefer jet, pipestone, and dolomite for their work. Loren Burns mostly does layered inlaid turtles.

The Bossie Quam family branch has a few carvers, all of whom work in a variety of styles like the rest of the Quams. Currently only Farlan and Paulette Quam produce many fetishes. They are especially known for their bears.

THE ANDREW EMERSON QUAM AND BOSSIE QUAM FAMILIES

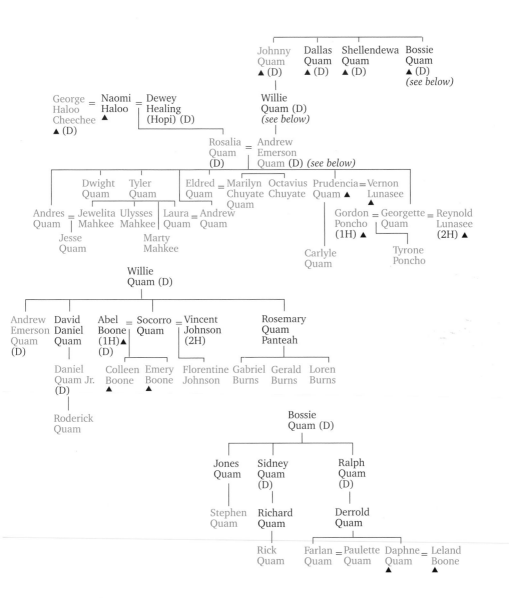

Jewelita Mahkee,
Picasso marble bear

Andres Quam,
dolomite bear

Ulysses Mahkee,
pipestone bear

Andrew and Laura Quam,
mother-of-pearl and turquoise turtle

Jesse Quam,
Picasso marble otter

Eldred Quam,
jet wolf

Tyrone Poncho,
variscite rabbit

Octavius Chuyate,
turquoise horse

Marilyn Chuyate Quam,
serpentine frog

Georgette Quam,
jade turtle

Rosalia Quam,
serpentine frog
(circa 1970s)

Rosalia Quam,
alabaster horse
(circa 1970s)

Rosalia Quam,
antler owl
(circa 1970s)

Rosalia Quam,
serpentine frog
(circa 1970s)

Farlan and Paulette Quam,
Picasso marble bear

Marty Mahkee,
serpentine bear

Rick Quam,
serpentine rabbit

Daphne Quam,
serpentine turtle

Stephen Quam,
Picasso marble turtle

Florentine Johnson,
Picasso marble turtle

Daniel Quam Jr.,
cedar bear

Gabriel Burns,
pipestone bear

Roderick Quam,
cedar bear

Gerald Burns,
pipestone wolf

Loren Burns,
mother-of-pearl
and turquoise
turtle

Carlyle Quam,
serpentine frog
on a leaf

THE LUNASEE, TSETHLIKAI, AND CHAVEZ FAMILIES

Two carving families related to the Quandelacys are the Lunasees (LOO-NA-SEE) and Tsethlikais (TSETH-LIH-KAI). Most carvers in both families produce a similar style of fetish that is somewhat realistic but not heavily detailed. Their diverse animals in a wide range of materials are all very popular. Vernon Lunasee and his brother Ronnie were the first active carvers in their family, starting in the mid 1980s. Vernon was influenced by his wife, Prudencia Quam. The two brothers worked with most of their siblings, in addition to a cousin (Fabian Tsethlikai) and an in-law (Terrence Tsethlikai). Several of Terrence's relatives in the Chavez family also make fetishes. David Jr. and Leroy Chavez were the first, shown by Herbert Him Sr. (Leroy's ex-brother-in-law) in the late 1980s and then passing on the knowledge to other family members. The Chavez style is a little more simplified than that of the Lunasee family. The three Tsethlikai groups in the family are only distantly related.

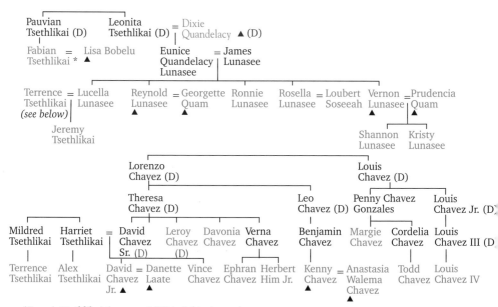

Francis Tsethlikai (see page 101) is Fabian's cousin.

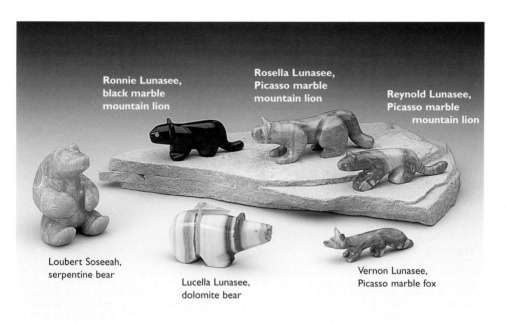

Ronnie Lunasee,
black marble
mountain lion

Rosella Lunasee,
Picasso marble
mountain lion

Reynold Lunasee,
Picasso marble
mountain lion

Loubert Soseeah,
serpentine bear

Lucella Lunasee,
dolomite bear

Vernon Lunasee,
Picasso marble fox

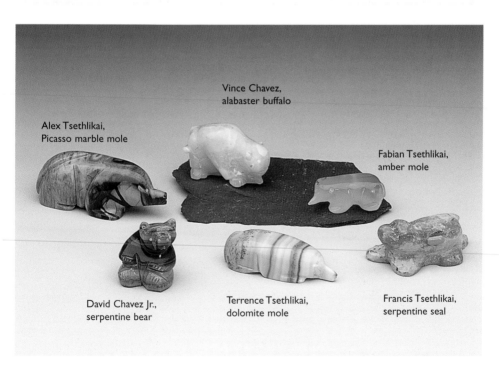

Vince Chavez,
alabaster buffalo

Alex Tsethlikai,
Picasso marble mole

Fabian Tsethlikai,
amber mole

David Chavez Jr.,
serpentine bear

Terrence Tsethlikai,
dolomite mole

Francis Tsethlikai,
serpentine seal

Herbert Him Jr.,
soapstone dog

Todd Chavez,
jet bear

Margie Chavez,
alabaster bear
(circa 1980s)

Kenny and Anastasia Chavez,
mother-of-pearl mountain lion

Ephran Chavez,
serpentine frog

Leroy Chavez,
marble bear

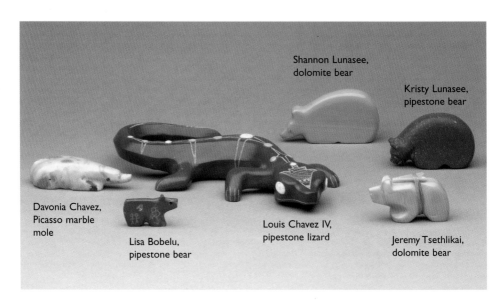

Shannon Lunasee,
dolomite bear

Kristy Lunasee,
pipestone bear

Davonia Chavez,
Picasso marble
mole

Lisa Bobelu,
pipestone bear

Louis Chavez IV,
pipestone lizard

Jeremy Tsethlikai,
dolomite bear

THE JOHNNY QUAM AND WESTIKA FAMILIES

The descendents of carver Johnny Quam form another important group in the large extended Quam family. Noted jeweler Annie Gasper Quam (died 2001) learned to make fetishes from her father, Johnny. (The work of her late sister, Ellen Quandelacy, and the Quandelacy family is discussed on page 89.) Annie's children also produce both jewelry and carvings. Their fetish style is somewhat reminiscent of that of their Quandelacy cousins, but in the main it is uniquely their own. Her grandson Todd Westika (WES-TIH-KA) was guided in his carving by his maternal aunt, Rhoda Quam, around 1990. His paternal uncle Myron Westika learned from friend Herbert Him Sr. Ellen Quandelacy's granddaughter, Karen Bobelu Hustito (BAH-BEE-LOO HOO-STEE-TOE), was encouraged to continue carving through marriage into the Hustito family, although her father had carved stringing and standing fetishes in the past. Because of the widespread nature of this group, their carving styles are quite diverse as well.

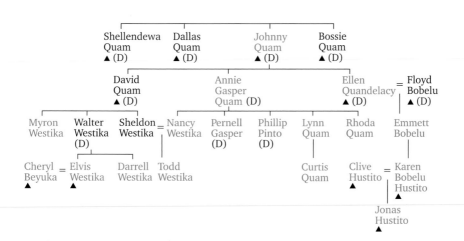

Rhoda Quam,
azurite coyote

Todd Westika,
Picasso marble buffalo

Lynn Quam,
rhodonite coyote

Annie Gasper Quam,
tagua nut turtle

Nancy Westika,
pipestone wolf

Myron Westika,
onyx bear

Darrell Westika,
alabaster bear

Elvis Westika,
Picasso marble
beaver

Jonas Hustito,
alabaster bear

Karen Hustito,
Picasso marble frog

Emmett Bobelu,
Picasso marble bear

THE HUSTITO AND LOWSAYATEE FAMILIES

The joining of the Hustito and Lowsayatee (LAO-SIGH-AH-TEE) families combined a wide range of carving styles. Alonzo Hustito (who died in 1987) was a noted jeweler who also carved fetishes for many years. His son Charles did both as well, starting around 1972. Herbert Hustito was the first family member to gain prominence as a carver, having learned from Dan Quam (see page 111) in the early 1980s. Herbert then taught his wife, Elfina, and together they helped other family members in developing their art. Most members in their immediate families do more realistic carving. Herbert's nephew Jonathan Natewa, however, makes a different kind of fetish since learning the sgraffito technique from his friend Russell Shack.

Elfina's cousins in the Quam family also do very streamlined work. Gabriel Quam was the first carver in this branch, starting in the late 1970s. Abby Quam Panteah (who began in about 1981) and her husband, Clayton Panteah, work at least partly together on most of their fetishes. Clayton is a phenomenal jeweler and started the inlaying of heartlines into their animals. Cousin Joey Quam was influenced by Colvin Peina's work. As shown on the family tree, this Quam family is related to the Quam families discussed previously, through Johnny Quam.

Alonzo Hustito,
serpentine frog
(circa 1970s)

Clive Hustito,
Picasso marble
buffalo

Cliverlie Hustito,
Picasso marble
Corn Maiden

Charles Hustito,
turquoise bear

ZUNI FETISHES AND CARVINGS

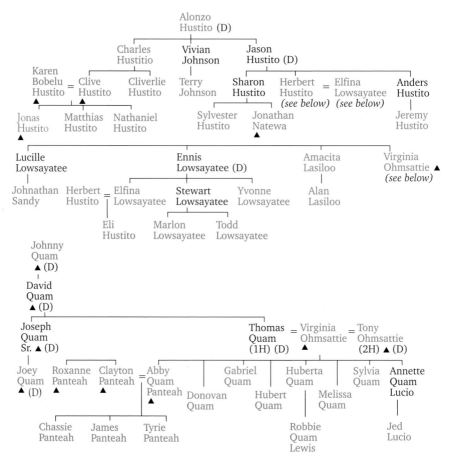

Alonzo Hustito (D)

- Charles Hustitio
- Vivian Johnson
- Jason Hustito (D)

Karen Bobelu Hustito ▲ = Clive Hustito ▲ — Cliverlie Hustito
Terry Johnson
Sharon Hustito
Herbert Hustito = Elfina Lowsayatee *(see below)*
Anders Hustito

Jonas Hustito ▲ — Matthias Hustito — Nathaniel Hustito
Sylvester Hustito — Jonathan Natewa ▲
Jeremy Hustito

Lucille Lowsayatee
Ennis Lowsayatee (D)
Amacita Lasiloo
Virginia Ohmsattie ▲ *(see below)*

Johnathan Sandy
Herbert Hustito = Elfina Lowsayatee
Stewart Lowsayatee
Yvonne Lowsayatee
Alan Lasiloo

Eli Hustito
Marlon Lowsayatee
Todd Lowsayatee

Johnny Quam ▲ (D)

David Quam ▲ (D)

Joseph Quam Sr. ▲ (D)
Thomas Quam (1H) (D) = Virginia Ohmsattie ▲ = Tony Ohmsattie (2H) ▲ (D)

Joey Quam ▲ (D)
Roxanne Panteah ▲
Clayton Panteah ▲ — Abby Quam Panteah ▲
Gabriel Quam
Huberta Quam
Sylvia Quam
Annette Quam Lucio

Donovan Quam
Hubert Quam
Melissa Quam

Chassie Panteah
James Panteah
Tyrie Panteah
Robbie Quam Lewis
Jed Lucio

Chassie Panteah, calcite snail

Jeremy Hustito, black marble snake

Tyrie Panteah, Mexican onyx frog

James Panteah, jet squirrel

Nathaniel Hustito, turquoise lizard

Matthias Hustito, serpentine frog

Jonathan Natewa,
black marble buffalo

Herbert Hustito,
antler eagle

Terry Johnson,
antler Corn Maiden

Sylvester Hustito,
black marble bear

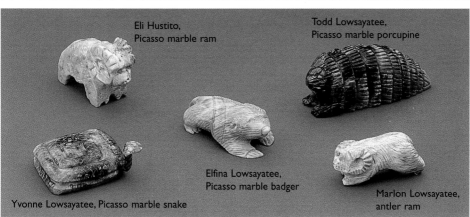

Eli Hustito,
Picasso marble ram

Todd Lowsayatee,
Picasso marble porcupine

Elfina Lowsayatee,
Picasso marble badger

Yvonne Lowsayatee, Picasso marble snake

Marlon Lowsayatee,
antler ram

Tony Ohmsattie,
serpentine (with augite)
owl

Alan Lasiloo,
black marble
bear on
dolomite base

Virginia Ohmsattie,
jet rabbit

Melissa Quam,
Picasso marble bear

Amacita Lasiloo,
tagua nut buffalo

Gabriel Quam,
alabaster
mountain lion

Huberta Quam,
alabaster bear

Sylvia Quam,
leopard stone
(jasper) rabbit

Robbie Quam Lewis,
travertine seal

Hubert Quam,
pipestone bear

Donovan Quam,
Picasso marble eagle

Roxanne Panteah,
serpentine bear

Joey Quam,
amber bear

Jed Lucio,
purple fluorite bear

Clayton and Abby
Quam Panteah,
Mexican onyx frog

Clayton and Abby
Quam Panteah,
tiger's eye bear

THE NATEWA, DALLAS QUAM, AND PANTEAH EXTENDED FAMILIES

Neil Natewa Sr. (NAH-TEE-WA) started carving in the early 1950s when he worked for trader Oscar Branson in Albuquerque while at school. He continued with Branson later in Tucson in the early 1960s but stopped producing fetishes by the end of that decade. Neil was famous for standing fetishes (especially bears and frogs), as well as bird stringing fetishes for necklaces. Unfortunately, according to Neil, his pieces were given to other carvers (including other Zuni, non-Zuni, and non-Native Americans) to copy, beginning in the late 1960s. Many of these copies have been fraudulently sold as his work. Neil also made jewelry with his wife, Shirley.

The children of Neil's cousins also carve, but each had a different teacher and thus produces diverse styles. LaVies Natewa learned from his wife, Daisy. Staley Natewa and his brother-in-law Travis Lasiloo (LAH-SEE-LOO) were guided by Lance Cheama (CHEE-AH-MA). Staley taught cousin Jedthro Mahkee. Among the nieces and nephews of Neil's wife, Shirley (through her sister Lorraine), some carve and some make jewelry. Fabian Tsethlikai, husband of Shirley's niece Lisa Bobelu, introduced most of his in-laws who carve to the art. Naturally enough, their fetishes resemble the Lunasee and Tsethlikai carvings.

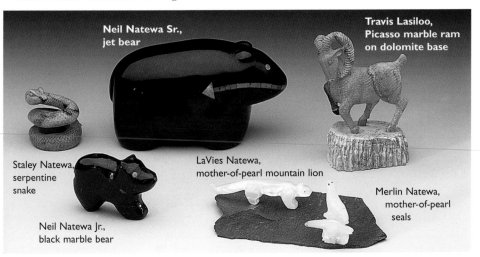

Neil Natewa Sr., jet bear

Travis Lasiloo, Picasso marble ram on dolomite base

Staley Natewa, serpentine snake

Neil Natewa Jr., black marble bear

LaVies Natewa, mother-of-pearl mountain lion

Merlin Natewa, mother-of-pearl seals

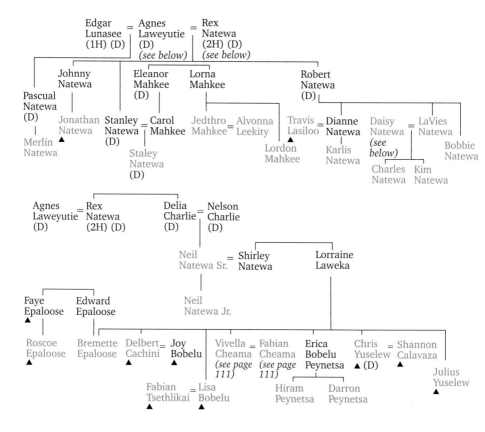

Daisy Leonard Natewa's extended family includes many artists whose work is more stylized or even harkens back to the "old style" in its simplicity. Daisy learned to carve from ex-husband Andres Quam (see the Andrew and Rosalia Quam family, page 97). Many other members were shown the process by Andres or his mother, Rosalia Quam, as well as Daisy. Rosalia's influence can sometimes be seen particularly in their hors-es. (The Leonard family's original name was Aisetewa [EYE-SEE-TEE-WA], which was changed to Leonard by the U.S. government because a member of the family had the first name Leonard.)

Whereas Daisy Natewa's family does primarily traditional carving, Fabian Cheama's family is the driving force behind contemporary work. (Fabian is married to Lorraine Laweka's daughter Vivella.) Fabian's half-brother, Dan Quam, started carving intricately detailed pieces in the early 1980s. Had it not been for him, realistic-style fetishes might

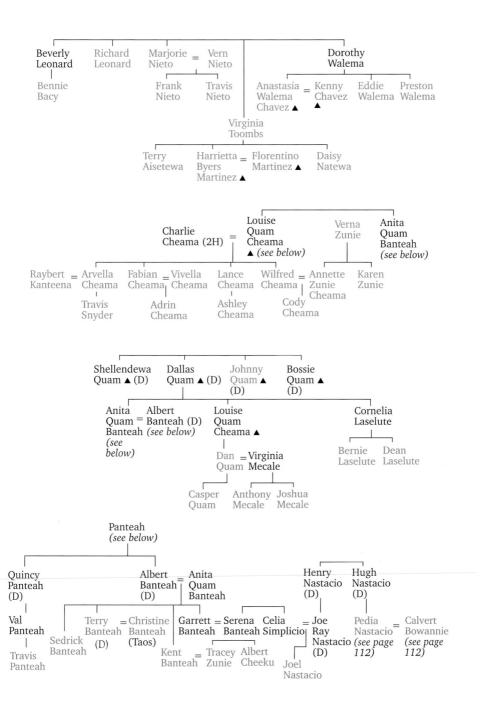

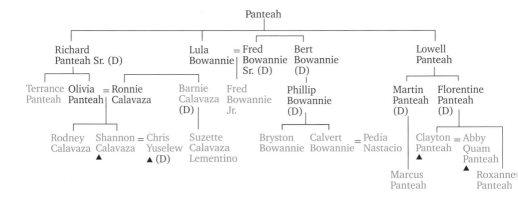

Panteah

Richard Panteah Sr. (D) — Lula Bowannie = Fred Bowannie Sr. (D) — Bert Bowannie (D) — Lowell Panteah

Terrance Panteah — Olivia Panteah = Ronnie Calavaza — Barnie Calavaza (D) — Fred Bowannie Jr. — Phillip Bowannie (D) — Martin Panteah (D) — Florentine Panteah (D)

Rodney Calavaza — Shannon Calavaza ▲ = Chris Yuselew ▲ (D) — Suzette Calavaza Lementino — Bryston Bowannie — Calvert Bowannie = Pedia Nastacio — Clayton Panteah ▲ = Abby Quam Panteah

Marcus Panteah

Roxanne Panteah ▲

not exist today. (This Quam family is also related to the previously mentioned Quams.) Dan showed the rest of his family how to do this exceptional work, and they have gained great fame and won countless awards since then. As noted elsewhere, they have shared their knowledge with many other carvers as well, including their wives, ex-wives, children, and Banteah cousins. This branch of the family creates a wide range of fetish animals, especially in Picasso marble and serpentine.

The Panteahs' cousin, Fred Bowannie (BOW-AHN-NEE), makes friendly looking animals primarily from local Zuni stones, while cousin Calvert produces a range of exotic and local animals.

The late Barnie Calavaza (KAH-LAH-VAH-ZAH) gained fame for his raccoons, whereas relatives Shannon and Rodney worked in the style of the late Chris Yuselew.

Julius Yuselew, Picasso marble bear

Hiram Peynetsa, black marble beaver

Chris Yuselew, Picasso marble dinosaur

Bremette Epaloose, Picasso marble turkey

Vivella Cheama, Picasso marble horse

Preston Walema,
Picasso marble seal

Bennie Bacy,
Picasso marble wolf

Richard Leonard,
calcite horse

Daisy Natewa,
malachite buffalo

Virginia Toombs,
bone horse

Eddie Walema,
serpentine turtle

**Florentino Martinez,
Picasso marble llama**

**Vern Nieto,
Picasso marble eagle**

Frank Nieto,
jet squirrel

Marjorie Nieto, serpentine rabbit

Travis Nieto,
alabaster bear

Terry Aisetewa,
sandstone bear

Dan Quam,
serpentine
mountain lion

Wilfred Cheama,
serpentine eagle

Dan Quam,
Picasso
marble bear

Fabian Cheama,
Picasso marble badger

Lance Cheama,
serpentine fox

Arvella Cheama,
amber hummingbird

Raybert Kanteena,
Picasso marble duck

Annette Zunie
Cheama, Picasso
marble badger

Karen Zunie,
variscite frog

Christine Banteah,
serpentine seal

Kent Banteah,
Picasso marble badger

Sedrick Banteah,
serpentine lizard

Tracey Zunie,
Picasso
marble otter

Terry Banteah,
Picasso marble horned toad

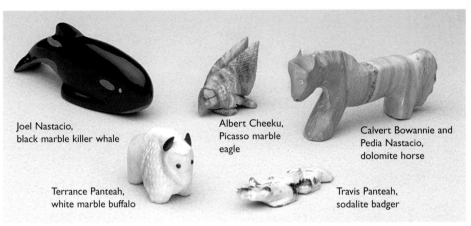

Joel Nastacio,
black marble killer whale

Albert Cheeku,
Picasso marble
eagle

Calvert Bowannie and
Pedia Nastacio,
dolomite horse

Terrance Panteah,
white marble buffalo

Travis Panteah,
sodalite badger

Fred Bowannie Jr.,
Nutria "sugar daddy"
travertine bear

Barnie Calavaza,
serpentine and
jet raccoon

Rodney Calavaza,
rhyolite bear

Suzette Calavaza Lementino,
serpentine turtle

Shannon Calavaza,
Picasso marble
bear

Bryston Bowannie,
marble fox

Bobbie Natewa,
antler ram

Johnathan Sandy,
alabaster whale

Kim Natewa,
serpentine bear

Karlis Natewa, serpentine ray

Charles Natewa,
alabaster bear

Adrin Cheama,
pipestone duck

Casper Quam,
serpentine dolphin

Ashley Cheama,
Picasso
marble fish

Travis Snyder,
Picasso marble bear

Verna Zunie,
Picasso marble seal

Cody Cheama,
serpentine frog

Joshua Mecale,
Picasso marble wolf

Anthony Mecale,
Picasso marble
mountain lion

Bernie Laselute,
Picasso
marble badger

Dean Laselute,
serpentine frog

Marcus Panteah, black marble snake

Jedthro Mahkee,
Picasso marble badger

Alvonna Leekity,
Picasso marble seal

Roscoe Epaloose,
Picasso marble scorpion

Darron Peynetsa, malachite lizard

Lordon Mahkee,
serpentine eagle

THE LEONARD HALATE FAMILY

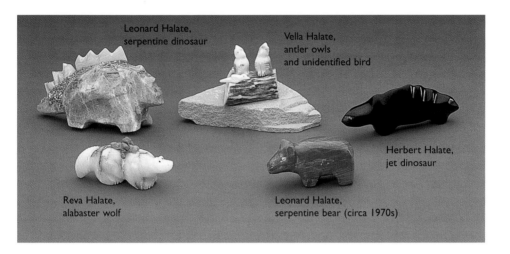

Leonard Halate, serpentine dinosaur

Vella Halate, antler owls and unidentified bird

Herbert Halate, jet dinosaur

Reva Halate, alabaster wolf

Leonard Halate, serpentine bear (circa 1970s)

The fetishes of Leonard Halate (HAH-LAH-TAY, died 2001) are easily recognized by most collectors. The whimsical feel and almost folk-art quality of his pieces are unmistakable. Leonard started producing on an intermittent basis in the 1940s. He focused primarily on jewelry-making in the 1950s before taking up fetish carving seriously in the 1960s. Leonard's unique style continues to influence some of his descendents' work. Others have developed a much sleeker and more rounded look to their fetishes (exemplified by the work of Herbert Halate and Justin Red Elk). The family particularly carves in antler, serpentine, jet, pipestone, and zebra stone.

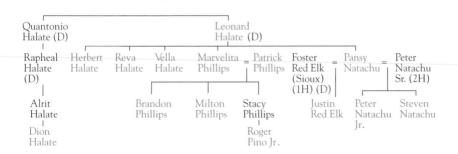

Patrick Phillips,
zebra stone
(marble) bear

Marvelita Phillips,
antler owl
and unidentified bird

Roger Pino Jr.,
antler bear

Brandon Phillips,
pipestone snake

Milton Phillips,
dolomite frog

Justin Red Elk,
jet otter

Steven Natachu,
pipestone eagle

Peter Natachu Jr.,
hickoryite (rhyolite)
mountain lion

Pansy Natachu,
jet bear

Dion Halate,
serpentine bear

THE SEPO PONCHUELLA FAMILY

Sepo Ponchuella,
Ojo rock (argillaceous rock)
bear (circa 1970s)

A jeweler most of his life, Sepo Ponchuella (SEP-O PON-CHU-EL-LA), who died in 1978 started carving fetishes in his later years. During the 1960s and 70s, he produced bears that were sometimes large and generally made of Ojo rock. For the most part, the art of fetish carving skipped a couple of generations in his family, but now several of his great-grandchildren produce fetishes. Other members of the family continue to make jewelry. Faylena Cachini (KAH-CHIH-NEE) was taught by her ex-husband, Eldred Quam, in the mid 1980s. She guided many of the other carvers in her family. Louise Wallace learned from her ex-husband, Fred Weekoty (WEE-KOE-TEE). Part of the family does very rounded fetishes, while others do fairly angular pieces. Most have a simple, more traditional styling.

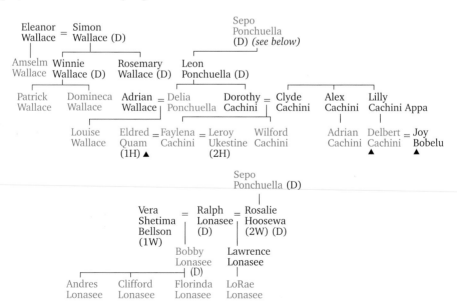

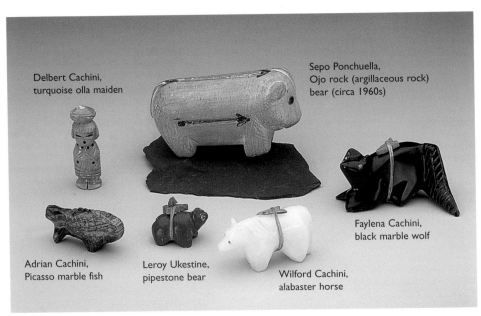

Delbert Cachini,
turquoise olla maiden

Sepo Ponchuella,
Ojo rock (argillaceous rock)
bear (circa 1960s)

Faylena Cachini,
black marble wolf

Adrian Cachini,
Picasso marble fish

Leroy Ukestine,
pipestone bear

Wilford Cachini,
alabaster horse

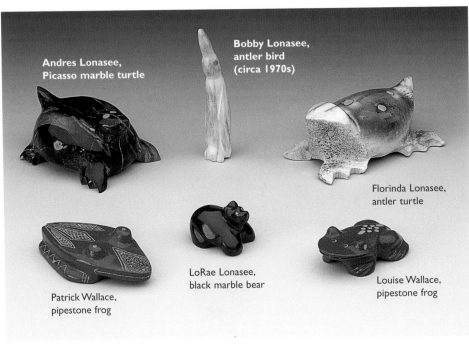

**Andres Lonasee,
Picasso marble turtle**

**Bobby Lonasee,
antler bird
(circa 1970s)**

Florinda Lonasee,
antler turtle

Patrick Wallace,
pipestone frog

LoRae Lonasee,
black marble bear

Louise Wallace,
pipestone frog

Amselm Wallace,
Ojo rock bear
(circa 1960s)

Clifford Lonasee,
antler owl

Delia Ponchuella,
Picasso marble pig

Domineca Wallace,
black marble bear

THE PONCHO FAMILY

Gordon Poncho,
dolomite lizard

Todd Poncho,
jet bear

Dan Poncho,
Picasso marble snake

Alex Poncho,
serpentine frog

Stephan Poncho,
pipestone snake

While few in number, the Ponchos are quite prolific fetish makers. In most carving families, the older members train the younger ones in the art. In this family, Gordon, a member of the younger generation, was the first to carve, starting in the mid 1980s under the tutelage of his (then) wife, Georgette Quam. Gordon's father, Dan, began producing on his own not long afterwards. All of the family create fetishes with simple clean lines. Some resemble old-style carvings, while others have a more modern flair. Their works are favorites with collectors.

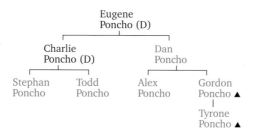

THE BICA AND KALESTEWA FAMILIES

Two very different styles of fetishes are produced by the Bica (BEE-KUH) and Kalestewa (KAH-LES-TEE-WAH) families. Simon Bica (who died in 1996) was the first family member to carve, but Rickson Kalestewa, his wife Nellie's grandson, gained the most recognition for his fetishes beginning in the late 1970s. Rickson works primarily in alabaster, producing carvings known for their humorous quality. Other relatives create fetishes in a similar style. Some family members on this side are noted potters, such as Rickson's grandmother Nellie and his mother, Quanita.

The Beyuka (BEE-OOH-KAH) family was originally most famous for its beautiful inlay jewelry work, until Cheryl started carving with the help of her husband, Elvis Westika. Cheryl then taught her brother Philbert and son Eli. The work of the Beyukas is generally more contemporary than that of the Kalestewas, and they often produce non-traditional animals.

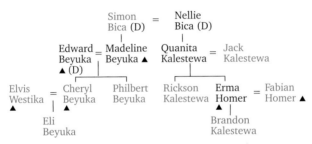

Simon Bica (D) = Nellie Bica (D)

Edward Beyuka ▲ (D) = Madeline Beyuka ▲   Quanita Kalestewa = Jack Kalestewa

Elvis Westika ▲ = Cheryl Beyuka ▲   Philbert Beyuka   Rickson Kalestewa   Erma Homer ▲ = Fabian Homer ▲

Eli Beyuka   Brandon Kalestewa

Simon Bica, alabaster bear

Jack Kalestewa, alabaster bear

Philbert Beyuka, zebra stone (marble) woodpecker on wood base

Eli Beyuka, azurite/chrysocolla bear

Cheryl Beyuka, green seasnail shell fish

Rickson Kalestewa, alabaster bear

Brandon Kalestewa, alabaster bear

THE SAUL YUSELEW FAMILY

Jocelyn Tsethlikai,
black marble bear

Randolph Yuselew,
turquoise mountain lion

Ricky Vacit Sr.,
jet bear

Avery Ohmsattie,
serpentine bear

Sherrie Ohmsattie,
marble bear

Ricky Vacit Jr.,
red dolomite bear

Saul Yuselew (YOU-SEE-LOU) first started carving fetishes occasionally as a teenager and then took it up seriously soon after his military service in World War II. He is basically self-taught and probably most famous for his bears, although he makes other animals as well. His style has changed over the years, but each era's carvings have their own traditional charm. His recent fetishes appear without eyes. Saul also made jewelry at one time. To the best of my knowledge, at about ninety years of age, Saul is the oldest Zuni carver still producing. His late brother-in-law, Harvey Bewanika (BEE-WAH-NEE-KA), carved as well and was also known for his bears. Note the inlaid "necklaces" that often adorn his fetishes. Saul has been teaching several of his great- and great-great-nephews and nieces to carve. Some of their work is easily confused with Saul's. His niece, Lorie Yuselew (formerly Lorie Bobelu), learned from her ex-husband, Keith Bobelu.

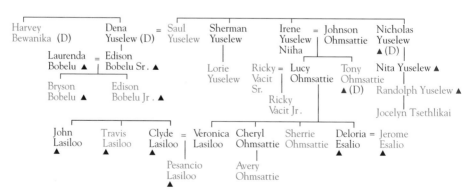

Harvey Bewanika,
serpentine bear (circa 1970s)

Lorie Yuselew,
black marble mole

Saul Yuselew,
jet bear (circa 1980s)

Saul Yuselew,
turquoise bear

Saul Yuselew,
serpentine bear
(circa 1970s)

Harvey Bewanika,
serpentine bear
(circa 1970s)

THE OTHOLE EXTENDED FAMILY

Gibbs Othole,
apple coral fox

Creating a truly different style of carving, the Othole (OH-TOE-LEE) family and its branches through marriage into the Esalalio/Esalio (EE-SAH-LAH-LEE-OH/EE-SAH-LEE-OH), Tsalabutie (TSAH-LAH-BOOSH-TEE), and Hattie (HAT-EE) families represent a new wave in contemporary carving. Showing more expressive elements along with surrealistic impulses, they produce whimsical creatures that charm the viewer.

Joey Quam was the first carver in the family (see the Hustito and Lowsayatee families, page 105), and he helped brother Alonzo Esalio and cousin Burt Awelagte (AH-WELL-AH-TEE) get started. Gibbs Othole, however, exerted the primary influence on the family's style. After visiting a friend in Albuquerque in the late 1980s, he picked up some Zia Pueblo alabaster and created his first fetish, an eagle. Since he started as a jeweler, it is not surprising that he incorporated an early parrot fetish into a broach, by placing it on a silver branch, in 1990. Friend Lena Boone helped gain exposure for his work and prompted Gibbs to use more exotic stones. Gibbs describes his work as traditional with a contemporary feeling. Expressionistic would be a fitting term. Gibbs encouraged Dee Edaakie (EE-DAH-AH-KEE) and cousin Albert Eustace (YOU-STAH-SEE, then a potter) in carving, in addition to influencing other family members' styles.

Jeff Tsalabutie began to make fetishes around 1992, having previously made inlaid jewelry. He worked with Gibbs Othole at the time and began making bears, then moved on to buffalo. His favorite animal to carve is now the mountain lion, and he especially likes to select turquoise and lapis for his creations. He also taught his brother Brion to carve in 2000. The family's work continues to be in great demand by many collectors.

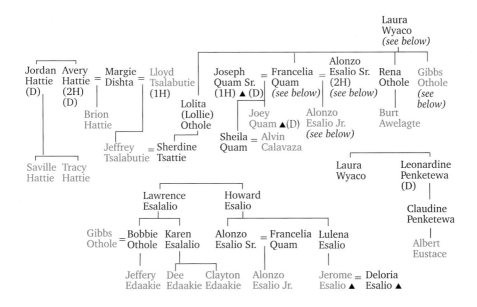

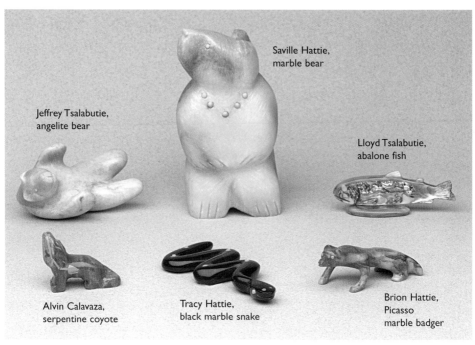

Jeffrey Tsalabutie,
angelite bear

Saville Hattie,
marble bear

Lloyd Tsalabutie,
abalone fish

Alvin Calavaza,
serpentine coyote

Tracy Hattie,
black marble snake

Brion Hattie,
Picasso
marble badger

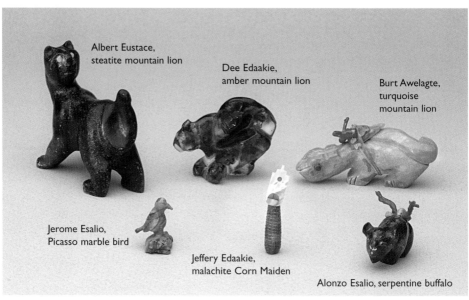

Albert Eustace,
steatite mountain lion

Dee Edaakie,
amber mountain lion

Burt Awelagte,
turquoise
mountain lion

Jerome Esalio,
Picasso marble bird

Jeffery Edaakie,
malachite Corn Maiden

Alonzo Esalio, serpentine buffalo

THE MAHOOTY, LASILOO, AND LAIWAKETE FAMILIES

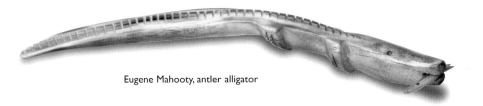

Eugene Mahooty, antler alligator

A group known for its emphasis on variety of materials, these interrelated families most-ly create highly stylized animals. While their carving is not generally detailed and often has sharp or only slightly rounded edges, these carvers will tackle a huge array of stones, wood, and shells.

The late Eugene Mahooty (MAH-HOO-TEE) first started carving in the late 1970s, followed by Lloyd Lasiloo (LAH-SEE-LOO) and finally Al Lasiloo in the early 1980s. They worked with then in-law Rodney Laiwakete (LIE-WAH-KEE-TEE or LIE-WEE-KAH-TEE), who helped spread the art to his brothers. The relative simplicity of their carving style shows off their stones to great advantage, especially labradorite, which must be cut at just the right angle to pick up the shifting colors and show its brillant "labradorescence." Al Lasiloo remarks that it is his favorite stone. All three Lasiloo brothers especially enjoy carving bears. Cousin Travis Lasiloo's side of the family (see the Natewa family, page 109) are the only naturalistic carvers in the clan.

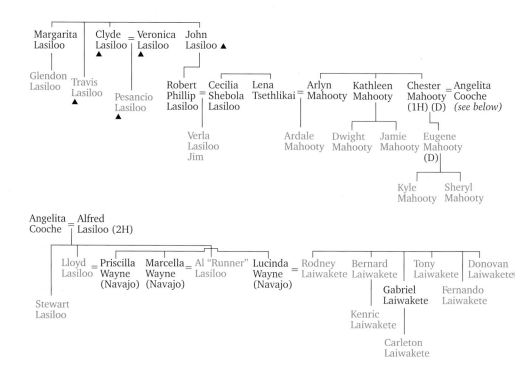

Margarita Lasiloo — Clyde Lasiloo ▲ = Veronica Lasiloo ▲ — John Lasiloo ▲

Glendon Lasiloo

Travis Lasiloo ▲

Pesancio Lasiloo ▲

Robert Phillip Lasiloo = Cecilia Shebola Lasiloo — Lena Tsethlikai = Arlyn Mahooty — Kathleen Mahooty — Chester Mahooty (1H) (D) = Angelita Cooche *(see below)*

Verla Lasiloo Jim

Ardale Mahooty — Dwight Mahooty — Jamie Mahooty — Eugene Mahooty (D)

Kyle Mahooty — Sheryl Mahooty

Angelita Cooche = Alfred Lasiloo (2H)

Lloyd Lasiloo = Priscilla Wayne (Navajo) — Marcella Wayne (Navajo) = Al "Runner" Lasiloo — Lucinda Wayne (Navajo) = Rodney Laiwakete — Bernard Laiwakete — Tony Laiwakete — Donovan Laiwakete

Stewart Lasiloo

Gabriel Laiwakete — Fernando Laiwakete

Kenric Laiwakete

Carleton Laiwakete

Travis Lasiloo, Picasso marble sea horse

Kenric Laiwakete, orange alabaster bear

Carleton Laiwakete, Picasso marble horse

Glendon Lasiloo, turquoise buffalo

Pesancio Lasiloo, Picasso marble turtle

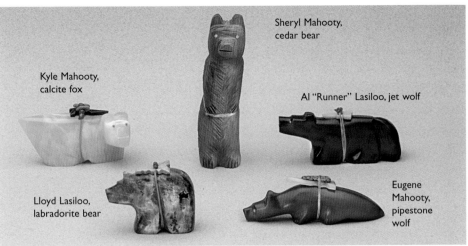

Kyle Mahooty, calcite fox

Sheryl Mahooty, cedar bear

Al "Runner" Lasiloo, jet wolf

Lloyd Lasiloo, labradorite bear

Eugene Mahooty, pipestone wolf

Dwight Mahooty, wood water serpent

Ardale Mahooty, Picasso marble bear

Jamie Mahooty, gold-lip mother-of-pearl wolf

Verla Lasiloo Jim, Egyptian marble and turquoise horses

Stewart Lasiloo, jet bear

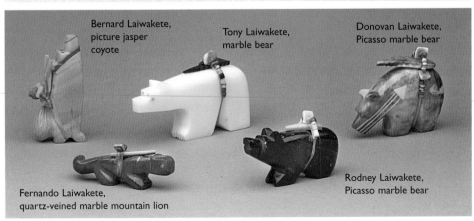

Bernard Laiwakete, picture jasper coyote

Tony Laiwakete, marble bear

Donovan Laiwakete, Picasso marble bear

Fernando Laiwakete, quartz-veined marble mountain lion

Rodney Laiwakete, Picasso marble bear

THE LAATE FAMILY

The Laate (LAY-AH-TEE) *family* primarily produces detailed carvings, but the extended family produces a variety of stylings. Pernell and Max (alternatively, Maxx) were the clan's first carvers of note, beginning in the mid-1980s. They made their own tools and began carving stones early on before turning to antler, which has long since been the family's favorite medium. They now use Dremel tools for greater detailing. They worked with nephews Elton and Derrick Kaamasee (KAY-YAH-MAH-SEE) as well as Lewis Malie (MAY-LEE) and Esteban and Ruben Najera (NAH-HAIR-AH). Esteban began carving around 1990, shortly after cousin Derrick, who started in the late 1980s. Esteban's interests lie in the gothic realm, including dragons, wizards, and skeletons. Derrick also started in stone (after creating paintings and pottery), then moved on to antler and now back to stone again as his preferred material. His subjects range from spiritual figures to wizards to insects. In addition, Derrick encouraged former brother-in-law Garrick Weeka (WEE-KAH) and Jerrold Lahaleon (LAH-HAH-LEE-OWN), as well as current brother-in-law Destry Siutza (SEE-OOT-ZAH) to carve.

Cousin Florentino Martinez started carving with his wife, Harrietta, in high school around 1991, first doing pieces with a simple style. He decided to try doing something more detailed like those he had seen from other family members. By 1996 his work had evolved to an incredible level of intricacy. His first detailed carving was a scorpion, and he still enjoys creating insects, especially in ivory, amber, and apple coral.

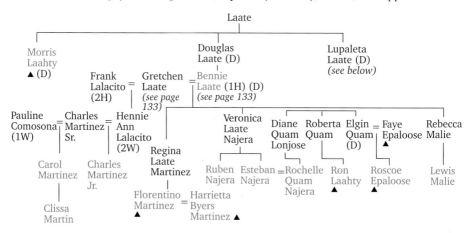

The other family branch primarily consists of noted artists who gained fame working in shell. Gale Lucio and Carlos Tsattie (TSAH-TEE) were the first carvers in this branch, although Randy Lucio may be its main teacher. He worked on shell carving with his wife, Adrianna Halusewa (HAH-LOU-SEE-WAH), and in-laws Yancy Robert Halusewa and the late Cellester Laate (died 2002), as well as cousin Carlos Tsattie (then an antler carver like cousin Willard Laate). Randy and Yancy have generally moved on to other stone selections that Randy says are actually harder to work than shell. While he started with bears, Randy has grown to especially like depicting human figures. Cousins of Ricky and Ron Laahty, this Laate family continues to impress with unique creations and a constant flow of new ideas.

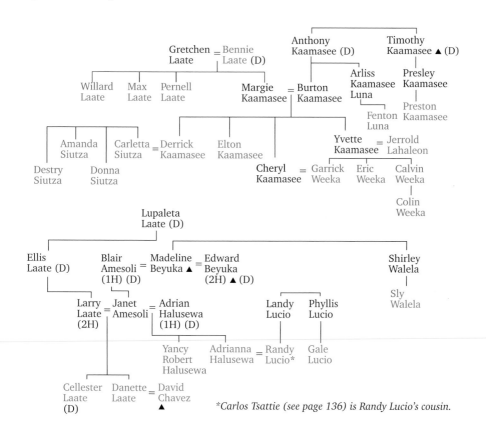

Carlos Tsattie (see page 136) is Randy Lucio's cousin.

Pernell Laate,
antler coyote

Derrick Kaamasee,
pipestone
Hercules beetle

Max Laate,
antler eagle
and snake

Willard Laate, antler owl

Elton Kaamasee,
antler eagle

Florentino Martinez,
verdite sea horse

Esteban Najera,
jet raven

Rochelle Quam Najera,
serpentine horses

Ruben Najera,
antler owl

Florentino and
Harrietta Byers Martinez,
Picasso marble bear

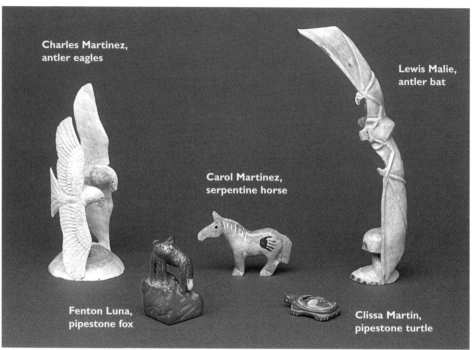

Charles Martinez, antler eagles

Lewis Malie, antler bat

Carol Martinez, serpentine horse

Fenton Luna, pipestone fox

Clissa Martin, pipestone turtle

Destry Siutza, antler bears

Jerrold Lahaleon, antler multi-figure

Preston Kaamasee, Egyptian marble bear

Donna Siutza, Picasso marble turtle

Carletta Siutza, wonderstone coyote

Amanda Siutza, pipestone turtle

Erick Weeka,
serpentine
beaver

Garrick Weeka,
antler eagle

Calvin Weeka,
Picasso marble
snake

Carlos Tsattie,
mother-of-pearl beaver

Colin Weeka,
Picasso marble hawk

Sly Walela,
mother-of-pearl anteater

Randy Lucio,
Picasso marble
maiden and child

Yancy Robert Halusewa,
mother-of-pearl owl

Danette Laate,
mother-of-pearl
Corn Maiden

Cellester Laate,
mother-of-pearl
mountain lion

Adrianna Halusewa,
gold-lip mother-of-pearl
turtle

Gale Lucio,
tagua nut buffalo

A GUIDE TO COLLECTING

Many people think they will collect only one or two fetishes, but this plan usually does not last long. A directional set is often the next group of items purchased. People usually wind up with a range of animals, often owning multiple examples of their favorites. Some collectors specialize in certain animals, some in specific carving materials. Collections of carving families is another popular mode. A few people purchase only "old" fetishes, whether that means ten or one hundred years old. Some believe that these are "true" fetishes. However, fetishes began to be carved for sale to non-Native Americans not long after the railroad arrived, well over a hundred years ago. Collectors who restrict themselves to exclusively "old" fetishes are also missing out on the exciting work of gifted contemporary artists.

If you do collect old fetishes, be extremely careful. The number of fakes on the market grows every year. Be sure a dealer can explain in detail why he or she believes that a piece is old. Do not accept something such as "because it feels old" as a reliable answer. Also be aware that some culturally sensitive pieces are meant to be communally owned by the tribe and used for religious purposes. These pieces should not be offered for sale.

Today a fetish collector can purchase almost any style, material, type of animal, or price range desired. An unfortunate consequence of the heightened interest in fetishes has been a rise in the number of imitation carvings from overseas, often sold as Native American handmade. The copies are usually very sharp-edged, a result of being sawbladed out quickly for cheap mass production. They are also frequently made of a so-called "block" material, which is nothing more than colored plastic cut into blocks for easy slabbing and shaping. Block plastic is patterned to look like turquoise, coral, jet, malachite, azurite, lapis lazuli, and spiny oyster shell, among other materials. Sadly, some Zuni carvers will also try to pass off block as the real thing.

The copying of Zuni fetishes by the Navajo has gone on since the mid 1970s and has become an issue. Navajo fetishes are sometimes misrepresented as Zuni, often through ignorance. The Navajo traditionally carved horse, sheep, and goat fetishes to protect their own herds and flocks. Many Navajo have purchased Zuni carvings of these animals for the same purpose. Larger wooden snake, human, and bird carvings were sometimes Navajo-made for religious usage. I have seen bear fetishes with other Navajo religious articles, but so far, all the older ones are non-Navajo in origin. Most Navajo fetishes (other than these just mentioned) attempt to capitalize on the commercial success of Zuni fetishes. Attributing Zuni meanings or directional and color associations to Navajo fetishes, although common, is inaccurate. The Navajo and the Zuni have different belief systems, and associating one with the other is a disservice to both. The buyer should be aware, however, that the Navajo have been strongly encouraged by Anglo traders to produce fetishes. And some do work in shops using mass production techniques.

After the initial stage of collecting, cataloging or note-taking becomes important. You may think that you will surely remember what the seller said about your fetish. But in a few days, that memory may fade unless the specifics were jotted down. Keep all your information together and accessible. Unfortunately, many stores and websites do not know who carved the fetish or even what tribe the carving comes from. So be careful. The seller should be able to tell you who carved the fetish, what tribe the artist is from, what it is made of (and guarantee that the material is real), and what the fetish represents. It is also helpful to get information on the artisan and his or her family. Sometimes retailers or individual sellers make mistakes and inadvertently mislabel or misidentify a piece. If this is a consistent pattern, however, find another source for your purchases. Merchants who are truly interested in fetishes strive to keep current on new carvers and

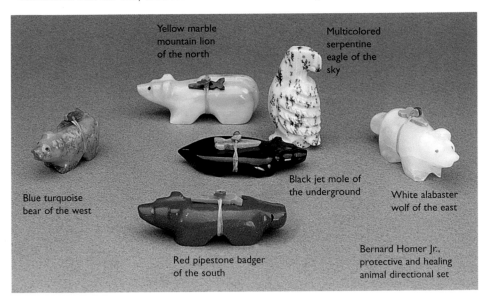

Yellow marble mountain lion of the north

Multicolored serpentine eagle of the sky

Black jet mole of the underground

Blue turquoise bear of the west

White alabaster wolf of the east

Red pipestone badger of the south

Bernard Homer Jr., protective and healing animal directional set materials. They carefully purchase their fetishes from artists or honest and accurate traders. And they are excited about fetishes and treat them as something special rather than just another commodity. Internet auction sellers should be held to some standards.

I have a simple rule of fetish selection: if the fetish "talks" to me, I buy it no matter what the animal is or which Zuni carver made it. People have the mistaken idea that they pick out fetishes. I believe that fetishes usually pick you out. I have seen countless incidents where people have walked past a case of fetishes, suddenly pulled one out, and said, "I guess this one's supposed to be mine!" This usually happens to people who had no intention of buying.

One final thing to remember: simply because a carver's work does not appear in this or any other fetish book does not mean he or she is not a good carver. There probably was not an example of that person's work available at the time the carvings were photographed. A good artist evolves a unique way of giving character to a piece. But most importantly, a carver's work is "good" if it appeals to you.

Dayton Yamutewa,
lepidolite eagle

BIBLIOGRAPHY

Adair, John   1944 *The Navajo and Pueblo Silversmiths*. Norman, OK: University of Oklahoma Press.

Bunzel, Ruth   1932 *Introduction to Zuni Ceremonialism*. Washington, D.C.: Smithsonian Institution, Bureau of American Ethnology, 47th Annual Report 1929–30.

Cushing, Franklin Hamilton   1883 *Zuni Fetiches*. Washington, D.C.: Smithsonian Institution, Bureau of American Ethnology, 2nd Annual Report 1880–81.

   1979 *Zuni: Selected Writings of Franklin Hamilton Cushing*. Edited by Jesse Green. Lincoln, NE: University of Nebraska Press.

Eggan, Fred and T. N. Pandy   1979 "Zuni History, 1850–1970" in *Handbook of North American Indians*, Vol. 9. Edited by Alfonso Ortiz. Washington, D.C.: Smithsonian Institution.

Ellis, Florence Hawley   1969 *Differential Pueblo Specialization in Fetiches and Shrines*. Mexico, D.F.: Anales del Instituto Nacional de Antropología e Historia, 1967–68, Sobretiro Septima Epoca Tomo 1.

Frisbie, Charlotte J.   1987 *Navajo Medicine Bundles or Jish: Acquisition, Transmission and Disposition in the Past and Present*. Albuquerque, NM: University of New Mexico Press.

Harbottle, Garman, and Phil C. Weigand   1992 "Turquoise in Pre-Columbian America," *Scientific American*, Vol. 266, No. 2.

Jernigan, E. Wesley   1978 *Jewelry of the Prehistoric Southwest*. Albuquerque, NM: School of American Research and University of New Mexico Press.

Kirk, Ruth F.   1943 *Introduction to Zuni Fetishism*. Santa Fe, NM: Archaeological Institute of America, Papers of the School of American Research.

Kluckhorn, Clyde, W. W. Hill, and Lucy Wales Kluckhorn   1971 *Navaho Material Culture*. Cambridge, MA: Belknap Press of the Harvard University Press.

McManis, Kent   2003 *Zuni Fetish Carvers: The Mid-Century Masters*. Santa Fe, NM: The Wheelwright Museum of the American Indian.

Parsons, Elsie Clews   1939 *Pueblo Indian Religion*. Chicago: University of Chicago Press.

   1964 *The Social Organization of the Tewa of New Mexico*. New York: American Anthropological Association, Krause Reprint Corp.

Rodee, Marian, and James Ostler   1990 *The Fetish Carvers of Zuni*. Albuquerque, NM: The Maxwell Museum of Anthropology, University of New Mexico.

Schumann, Walter   1991 *Minerals of the World*. New York: Sterling Publishing Company.

Slaney, Deborah   1993 "Zuni Figurative Carving from the C. G. Wallace Collection," Scottsdale, AZ: *American Indian Art Magazine*, Vol. 19, #1.

Stevenson, Matilda Coxe   1904 *The Zuni Indians*. Washington, D.C.: Smithsonian Institution, Bureau of American Ethnology, 23rd Annual Report 1901–02.

Tindall, James R., Annette Rogers, and Eric Deeson   1973 *The Collector's Encyclopedia of Rocks and Minerals*. Edited by A. F. L. Deeson. New York: Clarkson N. Potter, Inc.

Woodbury, Richard B.   1979 "Zuni Prehistory and History to 1850" in *Handbook of North American Indians* Vol. 9. Edited by Alfonso Ortiz. Washington, D.C.: Smithsonian Institution.

Zeitner, June Culp   1996 *Gem and Lapidary Materials for Cutters, Collectors, and Jewelers*. Tucson, AZ: Geo Science Press, Inc.

INDEX

INDEX

ACKNOWLEDGMENTS

This book could never have been accomplished without the help of so many people. My immeasurable love and gratitude go to my wife, Laurie, who almost 30 years ago rekindled my interest in fetishes and helped so much on this project. Everything worthwhile I have done in my life, I could not have done without her. Thanks to Corilee Sanders, Micheal Dunham, and Melissa Casagrande for their special help. Thanks to Sterling Mahan for initially pushing me to start this project; to Donald Sharp for his encouragement and information; to Pat Harrington, Joe and Cindy Tanner, Joe Douthitt, Alice Killackey, Boyd Walker, and Scott Ryerson for historical help; to Chet Jones, Greg Hofmann, Dick and Olga Anson, and Bob Jones for background on carving materials; to Rena Othole, Sarah Leekya, Denise Homer, Elaine Lesarlley, Kit South, Garrett Banteah, Darcy Cachini, Andres Cooeyate, and Lena Tsethlikai for information on carvers and their families; to Joan Caballero, John Kania, and Joe Ferrin for showing me the beauty of old fetishes; to Wells Mahkee for Zuni language guidance; to Darlene and Joe Foster for early support on this project; and to all the great people at Rio Nuevo Publishers and Treasure Chest Books for helping create and promote this work. Thanks to Bob Jeffries for so many years of help. Picture perfect thanks to Robin Stancliff for all the exceptional photographs that give beauty and life to these pages. A heartfelt "I miss you" and eternal thanks to John Stone, my trader mentor; Bill Adams, the man who taught me so much; and Larry McManis, my dad, for starting me down this long Native American trail. Great appreciation to Governor Arlan Quetawki for permitting me to do proper research on this project. Special gratitude goes to Fabian Vicenti and Shirley Leekela-Baca at the Pueblo of Zuni Census Office for assistance in putting together the family trees accurately and for their patience with my many stupid *"melika"* questions. *Elahkwa* to all the countless Zuni people who were so giving with their knowledge, wisdom, guidance, and spirit. Elahkwa to the many, many talented artists who create such beauty in their fetish carvings. And finally, to all the wonderful collectors and friends who have embraced my efforts and graciously helped me along the way, a humble thank you. Elahkwa.

ABOUT THE AUTHOR

Kent McManis became interested in Zuni fetishes in the mid 1960s when a trader friend presented him with his first carved bears. (He later discovered they were carved by noted artist Theodore Kucate.) Kent began his own Native American arts and crafts business in the early 1970s and met his wife, Laurie, when she came into the store as a customer soon afterwards. Laurie was the catalyst for their fetish collecting. Kent and Laurie own Grey Dog Trading Company in Tucson, Arizona.